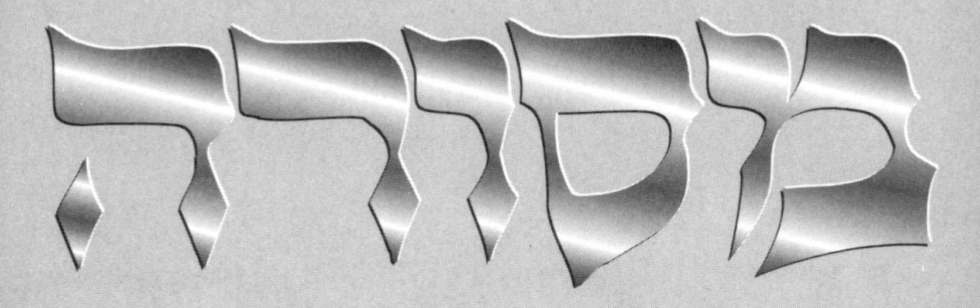

ArtScroll Youth Series®

Rabbi Nosson Scherman / Rabbi Meir Zlotowitz

General Editors

RABBI SHIMON FINKELMAN

BELOVED BY ALL

Published by
Mesorah Publications, ltd

Rav Avraham Pam – a life of Kiddush Hashem

FIRST EDITION
First Impression ... February 2007

Published and Distributed by
MESORAH PUBLICATIONS, LTD.
4401 Second Avenue / Brooklyn, N.Y 11232

Distributed in Europe by
LEHMANNS
Unit E, Viking Business Park
Rolling Mill Road
Jarow, Tyne & Wear, NE32 3DP
England

Distributed in Australia and New Zealand
by **GOLDS WORLDS OF JUDAICA**
3-13 William Street
Balaclava, Melbourne 3183
Victoria, Australia

Distributed in Israel by
SIFRIATI / A. GITLER — BOOKS
6 Hayarkon Street
Bnei Brak 51127

Distributed in South Africa by
KOLLEL BOOKSHOP
Ivy Common
105 William Road
Norwood 2192, Johannesburg, South Africa

ARTSCROLL YOUTH SERIES®
BELOVED BY ALL

ISBN:
978-1-4226-0522-6

Typography by CompuScribe at ArtScroll Studios, Ltd.

Printed in the United States of America by Noble Book Press Corp.
Bound by Sefercraft, Quality Bookbinders, Ltd., Brooklyn N.Y. 11232

ספר זה מוקדש

לעילוי נשמת גברא יקירא

ה״ה הר״ר חיים צבי בן ר׳ שלמה ע״ה
וויינברגר

Dedicated by

Mr. and Mrs. Gedaliah Weinberger

לעילוי נשמת

ר׳ שמואל בן ר׳ יששכר דוב פוקס ע״ה

ר׳ אברהם שלמה בן ר׳ יצחק גאלדבערג ע״ה

ר׳ שבתי בן ר׳ יהודה רייגבערג ע״ה

Dedicated by

Mrs. Serena Fuchs

and her sons Berish and Moshe

לעילוי נשמת

מורנו ורבנו הרב אברהם יעקב בן הרב מאיר הכהן פאם זצ״ל

Dedicated by

Yonah and Yisroel Blumenfrucht and families

לעילוי נשמת האשה החשובה

קילא בת החבר ר׳ משה מרדכי ע״ה

Dedicated by

Mr. and Mrs. Yosef Hoch

מכתב ברכה מאת האחים פאם שליט״א
בני ראש הישיבה זצ״ל
שנכתב לרגל הדפסת ספר הראשון

כבוד ידידנו הרב שמעון פינקעלמאן שליט״א

ראה ראינו הכתבים של קורות חייו ופעולותיו של אאמו״ר זצוק״ל שהכנת לדפוס. וניכר שהם פירות של עמל רב ויגיעה רבה לאסוף ולברר להכניס ולהוציא לסדר על סדר נכון ונשא. הנה הצלחת לצייר דמות דיוקנו של אבינו לא רק להיות זכרון לאלו שזכו להכירו אלא אף לאלו שלא הכירוהו.

דרך מיוחד הי׳ לו בעבודתו ובעודנו בחיים חיותו לימד דעת את העם ועל ידי ספרו של כבודו יהיו שפתותיו דובבות בקבר שילמדו ממנו בני אדם את הדרך ילכו בה ואת המעשה אשר יעשון להיות דרכיהם נאים ומעשיהם מתוקנים בבחינת כזה ראה וקדש וחלק יהי׳ לך בתוכם.

ואפריון נמטי׳ להנהלת ארטסקרול/מסורה ובראשם הרב ר׳ נתן שרמן שליט״א תלמידו של אאמו״ר ולעמיתו הרב ר׳ מאיר יעקב זלוטוביץ שליט״א על עבודתם הגדולה בחזקתם להוציא לאור דבר נאה ומתקבל.

בברכת יישר כחך

אהרן הכהן   דוד הכהן   אשר הכהן

TABLE OF CONTENTS

PREFACE

t is now three and a half years since the publication of *Rav Pam: The Life and Ideals of Rabbi Avraham Yaakov HaKohen Pam*. I am gratified that the book was very well received, and especially that those who were close to Rav Pam view it as an accurate portrayal of its subject.

That book, both in style and content, was written specifically for adults. After its publication, many people felt that there would be great benefit in adapting the material — especially the stories — in a new volume that would be geared for teens.

I am therefore grateful for having been able, with the help of Hashem, to write *Beloved by All*. While the book is based on the original work, it also contains new stories and photographs. I am hopeful that it will inspires readers of all ages, so that Rav Pam's shining example will light the way for them and their future generations.

I take this opportunity to once again express my *hakaras hatov* to Rebbetzin Pam. *Klal Yisrael* owes her an eternal debt of gratitude for the many years — especially Rav Pam's final years — when she stood faithfully at his side, caring for his every need. I am personally indebted to her for sharing her recollections with me in preparation for the original volume. May she enjoy many years of *nachas* from her family, in good health.

As with the previous volume, I undertook this work with the approval of Rav Pam's three distinguished sons, Rabbi Aharon Pam, Rabbi Dovid Pam and Rabbi Asher Pam. I am grateful to them for reading the manuscript and offering important comments and suggestions.

I am grateful to Rabbi Hillel David, שליט"א, who offered crucial advice in the early stages of this project.

My *hakaras hatov* to the noted *askan* R' Gedaliah Weinberger, a close talmid of Rav Pam, who recognized the importance of this project and encouraged me to embark on it. R' Gedaliah; Mrs. Serena Fuchs and her sons R' Berish and R' Moshe; R' Yonah and R' Yisroel Blumenfrucht; and R' Yosef Hoch have a share in perpetuating Rav Pam's great legacy through their dedication of this book. The above gentlemen were all close talmidim of the Rosh Yeshivah. By devoting themselves loyally to his causes and way of life, they bring honor to his memory.

My thanks to an anonymous donor who, recognizing the importance of this book, dedicated it in memory of הרב יעקב בן אליעזר ז"ל ורעיתו חיה שרה בת הרב אהרן ע"ה. Like Rav Pam himself, he places the cause above personal honor.

My thanks to Mrs. Gittel Bressler, secular studies principal of the Yeshivah of Brooklyn Girls' Junior High Division, for reading and commenting on the manuscript.

My appreciation, once again, to all those who shared their recollections of Rav Pam or their photographs for the original volume. They have a share in this book as well. I am grateful to all those who responded to the notice in *The Jewish Observer* to submit anecdotes for this new volume.

The original volume was greatly enhanced by many photos — reproduced in this volume — from the archives of Moshe D. Yarmish and Tsemach Glenn, both talmidim of Rav Pam. For this new volume, I owe a special debt of gratitude to Tsemach, who spent hours combing his archives for previously unpublished photos and for an appropriate cover photo. I am thankful that his efforts were successful.

R' Meir Levy and R' Reuven Kaplan, friends and neighbors of our family for many years, also enjoyed the *zechus* of living in close proximity to Rav Pam and seeing him often. I thank them both for providing a number of previously unpublished photographs for this volume.

It is difficult and probably impossible for me to properly express my *hakaras hatov* to Rabbi Nosson Scherman and Rabbi Meir Zlotowitz for all that they have done for me over the years. May I offer a *bircas hedyot* that they be granted good health and *siyata diShmaya* to continue their *avodas hakodesh* עד ביאת גואל. I am also grateful to Rabbi Scherman for his guidance throughout the various stages of this project; for reading and commenting on the manuscript; and for always "being there" for me.

ArtScroll graphics bear the imprint of the graphics master, R' Sheah Brander. My thanks to him, to Eli Kroen for the beautiful cover and graphics work; to Esty Goldstein and Chaya Suri Sternlicht and to the rest of the ArtScroll staff.

I am fortunate to count Avraham Biderman among my friends. I thank him for his efforts for this and other projects and for always being a good sounding board. My thanks also to his secretary Mrs. Danit Gantz.

My thanks to Mendy Herzberg, who coordinated the production of this book in his usual efficient and pleasant manner.

My appreciation to all the wonderful people at Yeshivah Darchei Torah, where I am privileged to teach, and especially to our Rosh HaYeshivah, Rabbi Yaakov Bender, and President, Mr. Ronald Lowinger. My appreciation also to all the wonderful people at Camp Agudah where I am privileged to spend my summers, and especially to Agudath Israel's Executive Secretary Rabbi Boruch Borchardt; our Director Meir Frischman; and Head Counselor Rabbi Simcha Kaufman.

I vividly recall Rav Pam greeting my father, עמו"ש, with a kiss when we came to the Torah Vodaath dinner tendered in the Rosh HaYeshivah's honor. May this effort at *harbatzas haTorah* serve as a *zechus* for my father and for the lofty *neshamah* of my mother, ע"ה.

My father-in-law's good cheer and perseverence despite difficulties, and my mother-in-law's devotion to him, are an inspiration to us all. May they be granted good health, long life, and much *nachas*.

Whatever I accomplish is to the credit of my wife, Tova, תחי'. יהי רצון שימלא ה' משאלות לבה לטובה.

I thank the *Ribono shel Olam* for enabling me to undertake and complete this project. May we be *zocheh* to keep the image of Rav Pam before our eyes, so that we may live lives of *Kiddush Hashem* and thereby merit the *geulah shleimah*.

Shimon Finkelman

21 Shevat 5767

CHAPTER ONE

A Life of Kiddush Hashem

It was a Friday afternoon when the phone rang in the home of Rabbi Avraham Yaakov HaKohen Pam. The caller was a young woman from his neighborhood who had recently given birth. "I am having such a hard time, Rosh Yeshivah," she said. "My newborn is a handful, the other children are not ready for Shabbos yet and I still have some cooking to do — and my husband does not come home from work for another hour! I called my doctor to ask if perhaps, in my situation, I could do certain things for my baby on Shabbos that I normally would only do on a weekday. My doctor replied, 'I am a pediatrician, not a *posek*. If you need to know something about *hilchos Shabbos,* I suggest that you call a rav.' When I told him that I did not know whom to call, he suggested that I call Rav Pam.

"So I took his advice, and that is why I am calling the Rosh Yeshivah."

Rav Pam responded in his usual soft and gentle way. "I am sorry, but I cannot answer you on the spot. I will be in touch with you soon."

In fact, Rav Pam knew the *halachah*; what the woman had asked to do was forbidden on Shabbos. To simply tell her, "It's *asur* (forbidden)," would have allowed him to hang up the phone and return to his learning or Shabbos preparations. But Rav Pam could not do this.

He understood from the woman's words and tone of voice that she was upset and feeling overwhelmed. If he would simply inform her of the halachah and wish her a "Good Shabbos," he would be leaving her with no plan for how to ease her situation. Rav Pam's great heart, which was fine-tuned to feel the pain and distress of every Jew, young and old, could not allow this.

Ten minutes after the phone call ended, the woman's doorbell rang. Rav Pam's granddaughter was there, along with a friend. They had come to help the woman with her Shabbos preparations. One girl bathed the children, while the other helped in the kitchen. A half-hour later, Rav Pam called the woman's home.

"How is everything?" he asked.

"Oh, Rosh Yeshivah! I can't thank you enough. The girls have been such a terrific help."

"Good, very good," Rav Pam replied. "As far as that question you asked, the halachah does not permit us to do such things on Shabbos."

"That's fine, Rosh Yeshivah. I only asked the question because I was feeling so overwhelmed, and was afraid that I would not be properly prepared for Shabbos. But thanks to the help that the Rosh Yeshivah sent, everything is under control and I am much calmer."

"... is it possible that Rebbi could pay him a visit?"

The talmid standing before Rav Pam had come to make an unusual request. The talmid's father had suffered a heart attack and was hospitalized. "My father mentioned to me," the young man had said, "that it would make him very happy if Rebbi would visit him. I know that Rebbi's time is very precious to him. But is it possible ... ?"

Rav Pam's time *was* very precious to him; he never wasted a minute. But to help lift the spirits of someone who is ill is certainly *not* a waste of time.

Delivering a shmuess in the beis midrash of Mesivta Torah Vodaath

There was one problem. As a *kohen*, Rav Pam was reluctant to enter a hospital.[1] He explained this to his talmid who, of course, understood.

But Rav Pam was not content with excusing himself from this mitzvah. If his visit was important to the patient, then he had to consider whether there might be a solution to the problem.

He had an idea.

He asked the talmid which floor of the hospital his father was on. "The second," came the reply. Rav Pam suggested that they set a time when the father would come to the window of his room. At that time, Rav Pam would be standing on the street below, ready to greet the man.

And that is what they did. At the appointed time, Rav Pam smiled as he waved to the man and offered his *berachah* for a speedy and complete recovery. The man was deeply moved by Rav Pam's visit and there was a noticeable improvement in his condition.

The Gemara (*Yoma* 86a) teaches: A Jew should study Torah, serve talmidei chachamim, deal honestly in business and speak pleasantly to people. If he does all this, people will say:

---

1. A *kohen* is forbidden to contract *tumas meis* (impurity imparted by a corpse) and therefore should not enter a hospital where the possibility of such *tumah* exists, except under certain circumstances.

Fortunate is his father who taught him Torah! Fortunate is his rebbi who taught him Torah! He who studied Torah — how beautiful are his ways and how proper are his deeds.

For 63 years, Rav Pam taught Torah to talmidim. However, even before he entered the classroom as a rebbi, he was already teaching others the beauty of Torah through his shining example of kindness and truth, pleasantness and humility. His life was one continuous *kiddush Hashem.*

Unruffled

One night, a talmid knocked on Rav Pam's door to seek advice in an important matter. Rav Pam, as always, greeted his talmid warmly, but explained that he could not meet with him at this time. Someone had called to invite him to a *vort* (engagement celebration) which was in progress. Rav Pam had attempted to decline the invitation, because his hectic schedule and dedication to his talmidim made it extremely difficult to attend such celebrations. But the caller had made it clear that it would mean very much to him if Rav Pam would attend, so he felt that he had to go.

Rav Pam had asked that a car be sent for him right away for the twenty-minute drive to the *simchah*. The talmid waited with his rebbi for the car to arrive. It never came. Finally, Rav Pam glanced at his watch, removed his coat and said with a smile, "I guess they forgot."

The talmid was amazed. Rav Pam had not wanted to go; he had only agreed because the caller had been so persistent. He had stopped whatever he had been doing and prepared to leave the house — all for naught. Yet, he was completely relaxed, not the least bit ruffled.

How does one become like that?

Rav Pam's every moment — literally — was devoted to fulfilling Hashem's will. In this situation, Rav Pam had done what he had felt was correct by agreeing to attend the *vort*; whether or not the car arrived was something over which he had no control. What was to be gained by becoming upset?

The Best Way to Celebrate

Rav Pam once related a story which illustrates how every Jew, in his or her own way, can teach others by example:

> *I knew an elderly couple when I lived in East Flatbush. I thought they were simple, ordinary people — but then I realized they were not simple people at all.*
>
> *Before their 50th wedding anniversary, their children presented them with a plan: "When you were married, you couldn't afford a hall or a catered affair. You barely had a minyan there! For your golden anniversary, we will make you the catered simchah that you never had, for the whole family and all your friends."*
>
> *A few days later, the parents asked the children to come over, and the father spoke. "All our lives, we could never afford to give tzedakah the way we wanted to. So what would you say if we did the following? Instead of a big catered affair, we*

will invite the children and grandchildren to our house, and your mother will make a meal the way only she knows how to. If it's okay with you, please give us the money you wanted to spend, and we will distribute it as tzedakah."

Rav Pam concluded, "When we marry off our children, we all look for *segulos* (omens) that will help assure happy lives for them. What better *segulah* can there be than to make a smaller, simpler affair, and use the extra money for Torah and *chesed*!"

A Tale of Two Names

Living a life of *kiddush Hashem* means being able to put aside personal desires for the sake of peace and harmony.

A couple who were blessed with their first child — a boy — came to Rav Pam for a *berachah* and some sorely needed advice. Both grandfathers had passed away; both grandmothers were living. The family custom was to name after only one person. Each grandmother had made it very clear that she expected the baby to carry *her* husband's name.

Rav Pam had an ear for everyone's troubles.

Rav Pam asked the couple a few questions and then told the

couple which name to use. He then asked the husband to dial the number of the grandmother whose husband's name would not be used. Rav Pam took the phone, wished the grandmother "*Mazel tov*," and offered his heartfelt blessings. He then told her that her husband, who was now in Gan Eden, would be greatly pained if his name were to be the cause of *machlokes* (strife). However, his *neshamah* would experience great joy if she would put aside her own wishes and allow the other grandfather's name to be used. Rav Pam told the grandmother that people want a child to carry a family name as a merit for the *niftar* (deceased), and in this case, the greatest merit would come from making sure that the family would remain at peace.

The grandmother said that she agreed to allow the other name to be used. Rav Pam blessed her warmly for her decision.

The couple visited Rav Pam soon after the bris. They reported that the only "problem" had been that when the other grandmother learned of what Rav Pam had said, she said that *she* would have "given in" to earn such a *zechus* (merit)!

Shameful "Fun"

Someone who truly seeks to live a life of *kiddush Hashem* will constantly examine his actions to determine whether they are pleasing to Hashem. Sometimes, seemingly innocent behavior is, in fact, forbidden. If only we would think before we act, we would realize this on our own. In his *Sefer Atarah LaMelech*, Rav Pam offers an example:

> *Many times I have seen adults play with children in the following manner: The adult snatches something from the child and hides it in his*

In his study with a young visitor

hand. When the child tries to take the item back, the adult switches it to the other hand or puts his hand behind his back, and this scenario is repeated again and again ... The adult continues to tease the child until the child bursts into tears, at which point the adult returns the item. He feels no remorse over what he has done, no regret for the pleasure which he has enjoyed from playing

At the upsherin of a talmid's son

this "game" — for what could be wrong with having some fun? In fact, this is very shameful behavior and involves numerous sins ...

I say that it is very shameful because of the cruelty involved. Anyone who causes distress to someone else, even for a moment, and derives pleasure from this, is guilty of a serious sin.

Similarly, Rav Pam condemned the practice of singing *grammen* (rhymes) on Purim that make fun of others. Of the Torah, the *pasuk* states: דְּרָכֶיהָ דַרְכֵי נֹעַם, *Its ways are ways of pleasantness (Mishlei* 4:2). To make fun of others is not the Torah way.

Rav Pam taught by example to be extremely sensitive to another person's feelings. Once, the door of Rav Pam's mesivta class opened and in walked a beggar asking for *tzedakah*. As Rav Pam withdrew some money, the beggar said something which made no sense, and which the talmidim found quite amusing. Rav Pam responded kindly to the man's remark, as if it was something to be reckoned with. After the beggar left, Rav Pam told the class that speaking with the man and acknowledging his opinions was a greater mitzvah than giving him *tzedakah*, for as the Gemara teaches, "One who gives a small coin to a pauper receives six blessings, but one who comforts him with words receives eleven blessings" (*Bava Basra* 9b).

His Whole Heart

In the last year of his life, Rav Pam participated in a parlor meeting to raise money for *kiruv* (Jewish outreach) efforts. Rav Pam attended not only to help raise *tzedakah*, but also to lend *chizuk* (encouragement) to the head of this *kiruv* organization.

He was in much pain at the time and the climb up the staircase to the home where the meeting was held was extremely difficult. Someone said, "I'm sorry that it is so difficult for the Rosh Yeshivah." Rav Pam responded, "To lend encouragement to a Jew is difficult? To sit at home is difficult."

A well-known organization asked Rav Pam to solicit a donation from a wealthy individual. Rav Pam had never met the man, but he made the phone call and was quite successful. Afterwards, the organization's president said to the donor, "Let me explain to you what kind of person Rav Pam is." "That isn't necessary," the man responded. "When he spoke, I felt that he was giving his whole heart to me."

One Friday afternoon, a man was sitting in a chair in a Kensington barber shop when Rav Pam walked in. This was

Leaving a parlor meeting escorted by his talmidim, Gedaliah Weinberger (left) and Rabbi Baruch Diamond

in his last years when walking was extremely difficult for him. He turned to the two Russian barbers and said in Yiddish, "My dear, good friends! *A Gutten Shabbos*!" and he left the store. He had made the effort to come to the shop simply to make two Jews from the Former Soviet Union feel loved.

A Ben Torah's Responsibility

Rav Pam taught his talmidim that as Jews — and especially as *bnei Torah* — they had a responsibility to live their lives with one goal in mind: to glorify Hashem's Name in this world. Wherever he goes, whatever he does, a Jew must always ask himself: "Is what I am about to do going to create a *kiddush Hashem* or, G-d forbid, the opposite?"

Rav Pam often quoted a piece of advice that the Chofetz Chaim imparted to his son, R' Aryeh Leib. The Chofetz Chaim would caution his son to avoid any action which could lead to disgrace of the Torah. Once, his son asked, "I am not an *adam chashuv* (distinguished personality) from whom others will learn — why must I be so careful concerning my actions?" The Chofetz Chaim replied:

> *Do not think this way. True, generally speaking, people may not look at you as a distinguished personality. However, if you do something improper, the same people will say scornfully, "Look how So-and so — a supposedly distinguished talmid chacham — is so lax regarding a mitzvah" ... Therefore, you must be extremely careful in all your actions.*

A young man related the following: Every morning, he davened Shacharis at a local minyan where the davening was at a slow pace, as he desired. One day, as he walked to shul, he passed a man standing outside another shul, shouting, "*A tzenter, a tzenter* (A tenth man, a tenth man)!" This man asked him to come inside to complete the minyan. The young man obliged but was quite upset by the fast pace of the tefillah; though he davened at a much faster pace than he was used to, he was barely able to keep up.

The young man asked Rav Pam: If he was asked again to be the tenth man for that minyan, should he oblige? Is a person obligated to lower his level of tefillah so that others will have a minyan?

Rav Pam replied: The young man was *not* obligated to sacrifice his own davening. However, the members of that

Writing the final letter in the sefer Torah written in his honor.

minyan would never understand how a *ben Torah* could refuse a request to help his fellow Jews form a minyan. Therefore, to refuse their request might create a *chillul Hashem*. He suggested that the young man walk to shul via a different route so that he would not pass that shul and encounter this problem.

The Sefer Torah Celebration

In 1993, in honor of Rav Pam's 80th birthday, Mesivta Torah Vodaath launched a campaign to write a *sefer Torah* in his honor. Three-and-a-half years later, in the fall of 1996, the *sefer Torah* was completed and a grand procession and celebration were held.

The *hachnasas Sefer Torah* celebration was the largest ever coordinated by Boro Park's 66th Police Precinct. The procession began at the home of Rav Pam's close talmid and Chairman of the Shuvu organization, R' Avraham Biderman, and it concluded at Mesivta Torah Vodaath in Kensington, a stretch of some 25 blocks. By police estimates, there were 5,000 participants.

At the conclusion of the day-long celebration, an exhausted Rav Pam, accompanied by family members, exited the Torah Vodaath building. As they headed towards a car, Rav Pam suddenly stopped and said that there was something he had to take care of. He returned to the building and told a member of the yeshivah's administration: "The maintenance crew worked long and hard today. They must be paid considerably more than usual. Please see to it that this is taken care of; if necessary, I will pay for this myself."

This kind of conduct, which causes everyone — including non-Jews — to respect and admire those who live by the Torah, should be the way of every Torah Jew.

When Rav Pam passed away, a non-Jew who had met him wrote, "Rabbi Pam's passing is a loss not only for the Jewish people; it is a loss for the entire world. I know."

Become a Talmid

Rabbi Yisroel Reisman, a distinguished rav and a *maggid shiur* at Mesivta Torah Vodaath, was a close talmid of Rav Pam. He wrote:

> *Who are the talmidim of Rav Avraham Pam? Our Rebbi's talmidim come in a variety of sizes and colors. Many are rabbanim and roshei yeshivah. Many others are businessmen or professionals. Some are government workers, even politicians.*

With Rabbi Yisroel Reisman

Rebbi's talmidim can be recognized by their p'nimius, their inner values. A talmid of Rav Pam shudders at the thought of taking money which is not rightfully his. He speaks politely to everyone, including immediate family. He has learned to react calmly when the going is tough. He loves Jews of all types and of all levels of observance. He wants a Jewish education to be available to all Jewish children, wherever they may be. He smiles and thanks his mother or wife after breakfast. Or, as Rav Pam put it, "Our talmidim have such ne'imus (pleasantness)..."

Let us read about the life of this great tzaddik, and in so doing, become talmidim of Rav Avraham Pam.

CHAPTER TWO

A Home of Torah and Chesed

Every *neshamah* is unique and special; no two neshamos are alike. We are taught that the secret of each neshamah is very closely connected to the person's Hebrew name. This was quite obvious in the case of Rabbi Avraham Yaakov HaKohen Pam.

While Rav Pam excelled in so many wonderful qualities, he seemed to represent, more than anything, the quality of *chesed* (lovingkindness) that Avraham Avinu symbolized; and Torah, as symbolized by Yaakov Avinu. For 63 years, Rav Pam was an outstanding, very beloved teacher of Torah. And he was someone who stood ready to help anyone in any way possible, at any time, and at great personal sacrifice.

Also, Yaakov Avinu represented *emes,* truth, as it is written, "Grant truth to Yaakov, kindness to Avraham" (*Michah* 7:20). Rav Pam was a symbol of truth in our generation.

No one is born a tzaddik; each neshamah that descends to the world is faced with many, many *nisyonos*, tests. Only by passing the tests that are sent his way can a person fulfill the mission for which Hashem sent him down to this earth.

A great rosh yeshivah once said that we will never know all the difficulties that the Chofetz Chaim overcame in order to become the Chofetz Chaim, the greatest tzaddik of his generation. Similarly, only Hashem knows all the tests that Rav Pam faced in his life in order to become the great *gadol* that he was.

But we do know one thing. The fact that he did become so great had a lot to do with the examples set by both his father and mother.

Rav Pam's Father

Rabbi Meir HaKohen Pam was an exceptional talmid chacham. From his youth, he displayed a great love for learning. When he studied at the yeshivah in Slobodka, he would not go to bed for the night without taking along a *sefer* such as *Ketzos HaChoshen*, *Noda B'Yehudah* or *Chiddushei R' Akiva Eiger* — and he would fall asleep in the midst of learning from the *sefer*. He would engage his friends in lively discussions to clarify the Gemara they were studying with a clear understanding.

He studied in other Torah centers as well, the last one being the *Kollel Kodashim* founded by the Chofetz Chaim in Radin.

Rabbi Meir Pam

Rabbi Elchonon Wasserman, the famous Torah giant who was martyred in the Second World War, was perhaps the Chofetz Chaim's greatest talmid. When he was already renowned as a Rosh Yeshivah in Baranovitch (Poland), R' Elchonon would return to Radin every Elul to spend the season of *teshuvah* with the Chofetz Chaim.

During one Elul, R' Elchonon approached R' Meir and asked if he would like to become his *chavrusa* (study partner). R' Meir accepted this offer; years later he said, "Our learning together was not all that successful. We only succeeded in covering the first three *perakim* (chapters) of *Masechta Succah*" — a total of 41 *blatt*, learned in little more than a month!

A recent photograph of the building that housed the Chofetz Chaim's yeshivah

Rabbi Elchonon Wasserman (center) at Camp Mesivta during his visit to America in 1938

Lifelong Attachment

Rav Pam would relate two stories about his father to illustrate his incredible attachment to Torah.

In his final years, when he was in his late 80s, R' Meir was legally blind. The only time he could learn from a *sefer* was at high noon on a sunny day. At such times, he would put his gemara on a windowsill and learn for an hour or two. The rest of the time he learned from memory.

Once, his son R' Avraham came to visit him and they discussed a Gemara topic. R' Meir asked his son to look up a comment of *Tosafos* on *Zevachim* 86a. His son looked but could find no such *Tosafos*. R' Meir insisted that it was there. His son looked further and was happy to tell him that the *Tosafos* was on the

Rabbi Meir Pam standing next to his son, R' Avraham, at the wedding of his grandson, R' Aharon Pam. R' Binyamin Wilhelm, the kallah's grandfather, is reciting the berachah.

next page. R' Meir began to cry, saying, "Look what happens to someone in his old age. He forgets his learning!"

The second story took place in the winter of 1968. R' Meir, who was then approaching 90, fell seriously ill and was scheduled to undergo surgery. Though he hoped to survive the surgery, there were no guarantees. Therefore, on the night before R' Meir was admitted to the hospital, he gave his son, R' Avraham, final instructions concerning various *tzedakah* projects.

The next morning, the two rode together in a taxi to the hospital. On the way, R' Meir told his son, "*Zog a vort* (Relate a Torah thought)." Rav Pam responded by quoting a difficulty asked by *Tosafos* in *Masechta Succah* and a solution to it found in *Sefer Aruch LaNer*. R' Meir gave thought to this solution and then responded, "I am not sure that this is correct." There was no time to discuss the matter further, for by then they had arrived at the hospital and went directly to the admitting office.

The doctors decided that surgery posed too great a risk for a man in such a weakened condition. After a few days of hospitalization, R' Meir underwent a very difficult procedure instead of surgery. When he was brought back to his room, he was pale and appeared alarmingly weak, just barely alive. Rav Pam, who had been waiting in the room, was frightened by his father's appearance.

R' Meir motioned with his finger that his son should come to the head of his bed. Rav Pam's heart was pounding, for he feared that his father wanted to relate some final instructions before he departed this world. Rav Pam bent down to hear what his father would say.

"Who said this?" his father whispered.

"I don't understand," Rav Pam replied.

"Taxi!" R' Meir whispered.

"Ah!" Rav Pam replied knowingly, "the solution of the *Aruch LaNer* which we discussed in the taxi?"

"Yes," his father whispered, "I have thought the matter through well. He is not right."

In fact, there are *Acharonim* who disagree with the *Aruch LaNer*'s explanation. That Rav Meir Pam could be occupied with such thoughts at such a time is testimony to his great love of Torah.

Rav Pam's Mother

Rav Pam's mother, Rebbetzin Rochel Leah Pam, was the daughter of the Shedlitzer Rav, Rabbi Shimon Dov Analik, author of *Imrei Rashad* and *Orach Mishpat*. He was renowned as a *gaon* (Torah genius) and tzaddik in an era when Eastern Europe was a bastion of Torah greatness.

In an address to talmidim following his mother's passing, Rav Pam said, "A word of *lashon hara* never escaped my mother's lips. It seems to me, though, that she did not have to work on *shemiras halashon* (guarding one's tongue), for she loved people so much that she simply did not pay attention to their faults."

Rav Pam also related:

> *I recall that in my youth when we lived in Lithuania, there was a woman who had become mentally ill, a result of personal suffering and depression. They called her "Rivkah the Meshugeneh (the Insane One)." Her appearance was frightening. From time to time, she would visit my mother, of blessed memory, the town's Rebbetzin. My mother listened to her patiently and with rapt attention. My mother would respond to her with words that touched her heart and soothed her spirit.*

No matter how difficult her situation was, Rebbetzin Pam never complained. She once explained why: "If I complain, I might convey an impression that things are worse than they really are and people will sympathize with me for a situation that was not as bad as they thought; this would be untruthful on my part."

Rav Pam once spoke to his talmidim about his mother's beautiful *midos*:

> *She lived some 90 years and never did I hear her speak in a way which was not fit for people*

of exceptional honor. Certainly, she never said to anyone, including her own children, something like, "You fool!" or similar talk. Her speech was elegant, as befitted her exceptionally fine character. It was simply impossible for an unrefined word to come from her lips.

Over the course of her long life, she experienced difficulties, but through everything, she never exhibited anger. Never did she say something which she later regretted.

She never lost control of her emotions. True, Chazal tell us that a person is not held accountable for something he might say in a moment of great anguish. My mother, however, was always in control of herself, in moments of ecstasy and in moments of pain.

My father, of blessed memory, was on his deathbed on Chol HaMoed Pesach, a few days before he departed this world. My son Dovid, who was very close to my father, came to visit him. When he entered my parents' bedroom and saw my father looking deathly ill, his body connected to intravenous and other life-saving devices, tears welled up in my son's eyes and he turned to leave. He passed through the kitchen where my mother was sitting, but overcome with emotion, he could only manage to say "A gutten Moed," and then headed down the stairs.

My mother had noticed his tears. She went to the steps and called down to him, "Dovid, Dovid! Whatever will be, will be, but today is yom tov and we must be b'simchah (happy)!"

At a family wedding (clockwise): Rav Pam, Rabbi Asher Pam, the chassan, unknown, Rabbi Dovid Pam, Rabbi Yisroel Belsky

We see that the home of Rav Meir and Rebbetzin Rachel Leah Pam was one of *ahavas haTorah*, *ahavas Yisrael*, and exceptional *midos*, an ideal atmosphere in which a future Torah leader could develop.

CHAPTER THREE

The Road to Greatness

Rav Pam was born on 9 Tammuz 5673 (1913). The Ponovezher Rav, Rabbi Yosef Shlomo Kahaneman, was his *sandak*.

He would refer to his home town of Salok, where his father served as Rav, as a "a one-horse town." There was a town square and all the houses were built around it. The Jews of the village were steeped in Torah and service of Hashem.

There was no yeshivah in the town; by the time Avraham turned 10, his parents were left with no choice but to send him to Yeshivah Eitz Chaim in Rakaschok. The yeshivah building had no electricity, so the boys learned by candlelight. The older students got whole candles while the younger ones, such as Avraham Pam, made do with candle stubs.

The Ponovezher Rav

In Elul 5683 (1923), a *maggid shiur* at the yeshivah, Rabbi Avraham M. Weiner, wrote to Avraham's parents about their son's progress:

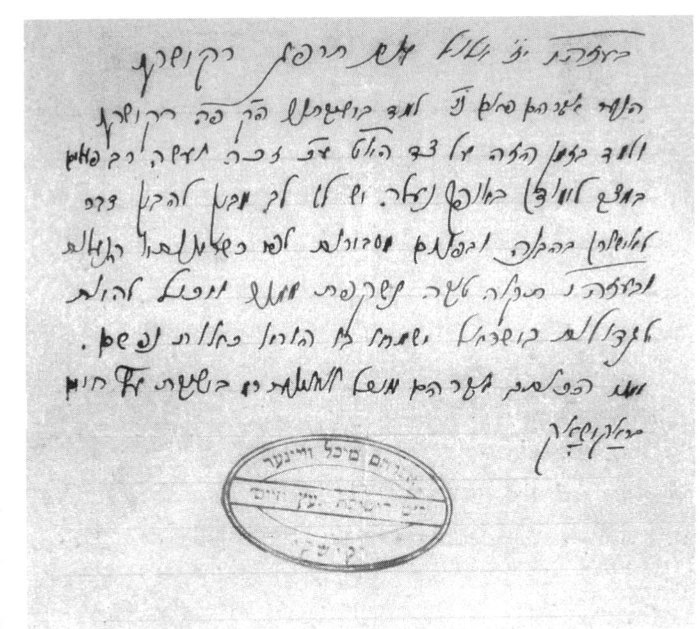

Letter from Rabbi Avraham M. Weiner to Rav Pam's parents, dated 17 Elul, 5683 (1923)

He learned exceptionally well and therefore made great strides in his learning. He possesses an understanding heart to comprehend a matter correctly ... With the help of Hashem, a bright future awaits him, and he can attain greatness in Israel. His parents can rejoice over him ...

Special Opportunity

When Avraham returned home for summer vacation, an opportunity to remain in Salok presented itself.

A yeshivah student in his 20s from the Kletzk Yeshivah came to Salok. He was suffering from asthma and doctors had advised him to spend an extended period in a rural area where he could inhale fresh country air. The young man was a genuine talmid chacham and R' Meir Pam, along with two other men, arranged for the student to become their sons' full-time rebbi.

The bachur insisted on teaching the boys *Chullin*, a difficult *masechta* dealing with *shechitah* (slaughtering) and related *halachos*. Few learn this *masechta* before the age of 20. The young man and his three talmidim would study together from morning until night; the bachur went so far as to take his young talmidim to the local slaughterhouse for a demonstration of many of the facts and laws that they were learning.

Once, on the Shabbos before Rosh Chodesh, the bachur said to the three boys: "I'm going to ask you a question and I want you to think before you answer. In *Rosh Chodesh 'Bentchen'* (the Blessing for the New Month), we ask for a life that has so many good qualities. Which request in this blessing is the best of all?"

Young Avraham replied instantly, "[May You give us] a life in which we will have love of Torah and fear of Heaven."

His rebbi replied, "I disagree. The best request of all is, '[May You give us] a life in which Hashem fulfills our heartfelt requests for the good.' "

"But can one really be sure that what he desires in his heart is truly best for him?" Avraham responded. "On the other hand, love of Torah and fear of Heaven are *certainly* correct and most important requests."

With Reb Yaakov

At around age 12, Avraham became a talmid at Yeshivah Ateres Zvi in Kovno, which was across the bridge from Slobodka. He was short and of slight build and appeared younger than his age. As he related in later years, this was actually a blessing. The *Haskalah* (so-called Enlightenment) movement had wreaked great damage among the Jewish communities of Europe, and the yeshivah world had not been spared. In Ateres Zvi, there was a group of bachurim who had been influenced by *maskilim* ("enlightened ones") and they would sit together and discuss their false beliefs. When Avraham Yaakov Pam would walk by, they would tell him, "Go away — you're too young for this."

During the week, he, like other students of the yeshivah, made the rounds of local Jewish homes to eat his meals. On Shabbos, the yeshivah arranged for each talmid to eat with a specific family. It was young Avraham's good fortune to eat his Shabbos meals with the family of Rabbi Yaakov Kamenetsky, who was then a member of the Slobodka kollel. Decades later, Rav Pam would renew this relationship when Reb Yaakov served as Rosh Yeshivah of Mesivta Torah Vodaath and,

With Rabbi Yaakov Kamenetsky in Camp Ohr Shraga

together with Rabbi Moshe Feinstein, was the acknowledged leader of America's yeshivah world. It was said that Rav Pam's passion for truth mirrored that of Reb Yaakov, and undoubtedly, in their many years together in Torah Vodaath, Rav Pam learned from Reb Yaakov's brilliant way of dealing with people and offering advice.

Torah Vodaath

In 1925, after several years of poverty and harrassment at the hands of Communist authorities, Rav Meir Pam came to the United States. There, he served as a rebbi in Yeshivas Rabbeinu Chaim Berlin and as Rav of the Beis Medrash HaGadol in Brownsville, Brooklyn. It would be two years before his family could join him on these shores.

Avraham's bar-mitzvah was celebrated without his father. Soon after, the family journeyed to America. Avraham became

This photograph, taken of Rav Pam upon his becoming a bar mitzvah, was sent to his father and his maternal grandmother, both of whom could not be present to celebrate with him.

a talmid in the beis midrash of Mesivta Torah Vodaath, then the only yeshivah of higher learning in Brooklyn. He was to remain a part of the yeshivah for the rest of his life.

Rav Pam once explained to his sons how he was able to join the beis midrash at the age of 14. He was ahead of the other boys because in European yeshivos there were no secular studies. In Europe, he had devoted himself fully to Torah learning, and thus was ready to enter beis midrash at a very young age.

Rav Pam was greatly influenced by the legendary founder and Menahel of Mesivta Torah Vodaath, Rabbi Shraga Feivel Mendlowitz. R' Shraga Feivel, who insisted on being known as "Mister Mendlowitz," was an outstanding talmid chacham

Rabbi Shraga Feivel Mendlowitz

and visionary. He possessed a burning desire to spread Torah throughout the length and breadth of America. Though R' Shraga Feivel succeeded beyond anyone's dreams, he remained the same humble tzaddik who fled from honor as from a fire.

At a *yahrtzeit* gathering for R' Shraga Feivel, Rav Pam spoke movingly of "the rebbi under whom I developed from my youth, and who later brought me into the work of the Mesivta [as a *maggid shiur*], where I taught under his guidance and influence." He added, "The relationship which I had with the Rebbi, *zichrono l'verachah*, was a close one and lasted some twenty years."

Rabbi Moshe Dov Ber Rivkin

Rabbi Moshe Dov Ber Rivkin, originally of Jerusalem, also had a great impact on young Avraham Pam. In 1929, R' Shraga Feivel appointed Rav Rivkin to serve as the Mesivta's Menahel.

Rav Pam once recalled:

I was a young bachur in Torah Vodaath when HaGaon Rav Rivkin, זצ"ל*, came to the yeshivah from Eretz Yisrael and became Menahel at that time. He tested me in*

Rabbi Menachem Manis Mandel greeting Rav Pam at a Torah Vaddath dinner at which Rav Pam was Guest of Honor

[Masechta] Kesubos and I was נוֹשֵׂא חֵן *(found favor) with him. In succeeding years, when I became a ninth-grade rebbi in the Mesivta, Rav Rivkin was very much mekarev me (drew me close) and offered me encouragement — and this meant very much to me."*

In the 1930s, Rabbi Menachem Manis Mandel, late Menahel of Yeshivah of Brooklyn, was standing on the street with Rav Rivkin when Avraham Pam walked by. *"Ehr vakst grois* (He is becoming great)," said Rav Rivkin.

Rav Dovid Leibowitz

When Rav Pam entered Mesivta Torah Vodaath, its beis midrash was led by the *gaon* Rabbi Dovid Leibowitz. R' Dovid was a great-nephew of the Chofetz Chaim,

Rabbi Dovid Leibowitz

and before coming to America had been an outstanding member of the famed Kovno Kollel. Rav Pam would always consider R' Dovid his *rebbi muvhak* (primary Torah teacher), saying that his approach to learning came from R' Dovid. He attended R' Dovid's daily *"blatt shiur"* for one year, and for the next five or six years remained in the Torah Vodaath beis midrash where he attended R' Dovid's weekly *"shiur klali."* During those years, he would engage his rebbi in Talmudic discussion, and in this way continued to gain in his approach to Gemara study.

Avraham was considered one of the yeshivah's "stars," a student who combined *amkus* (depth in learning) with unusual *midos*. His lifelong friend and colleague, Rabbi Nesanel Quinn, recalled: "He was the youngest in the class and the best in the

Rav Pam, youngest in the class, standing behind his rebbi, Rav Dovid Leibowitz

Rav Pam and Rav Nesanel Quinn in the beis midrash of Mesivta Torah Vodaath.

class — but he never sought any sort of recognition for this. This is how he was throughout his life."

"Rav Pam"

At age 19, Avraham Pam embarked on a two-year study program to master the four sections of *Shulchan Aruch* (Code of Jewish Law), with the major commentaries. While he spent some of his time learning with a *chavrusa* (study partner), he would study alone for long periods of time and with great concentration — an important but unusual ability.

Unusually humble, Rav Pam rarely spoke about his own achievements. However, he once told a close talmid who asked him about those two years, "I didn't eat or sleep," meaning, he ate and slept the bare miminum and used all the remaining time for Torah. The talmid exclaimed, "Rebbi! Perhaps we

Learning in the beis midrash of Mesivta Torah Vodaath

could organize a similar *chabura* (group) with the same goal in mind?" Rav Pam replied, "I cannot find the words to describe to you the kind of *hasmadah* (diligence) with which we learned during those years."

Avraham Pam and two friends were tested to receive *semichah* (rabbinic ordination) by three renowned rabbanim: Rabbi Moshe Binyamin Tomashov, the senior rav in Brownsville, Brooklyn; Rabbi Yaakov Kantrowitz (Rav of Trenton, New Jersey), who succeeded Rabbi Dovid Leibowitz as Rosh Yeshivah of Torah Vodaath;[1] and Rabbi Yehudah Leib Graubart, a distinguished rav in Toronto who was visiting New York at that time.

At around that time, R' Meir Pam remarked, "People say that I am a *lamdan* (one who has a deep understanding of Gemara), and I say that I have a son who is an *adam gadol* (great Torah personality)!"

1. In 1933, Reb Dovid left Torah Vodaath and founded Yeshivah Chofetz Chaim. Upon his passing, he was succeeded by his illustrious son, Rabbi Henoch Leibowitz, שליט"א.

A Blessing in Disguise

In America in the 1930s, the concept of kollel did not exist. A young man who hoped to marry had to have a means of supporting his family. Thus, in 1936, Rav Pam sought a position, but none were available at Torah Vodaath.

Fluent in a number of languages, he applied for a position as a court interpreter. He was highly qualified for the post and of all the applicants, he scored highest on the written exam. However, the judge in charge of hiring took his own nephew for the post.

He then applied for a rabbinical position in a small Pennsylvania community. It was arranged that he would go there for a "tryout"; he was to take a bus from Port Authority in Manhattan. As a rule, Rav Pam was very punctual, but this time he missed the bus by minutes. The tryout was never rescheduled.

Decades later, Rav Pam remarked that he was eternally grateful to Hashem for having led him along the path which allowed him to be a teacher of Torah all his life. He elaborated:

> *When a person misses a bus for a "tryout," the natural reaction is to feel terrible. "Oh, I've missed my chance, my opportunity!" he thinks. And I may have felt that way at the time. Years later, when I became a rebbi in Torah Vodaath and then a rosh yeshivah, I could look back and see what a great chesed the Ribono shel Olam had done for me by causing me to miss the bus.*
>
> *One should never feel bad when an opportunity does not work out, for he never knows what lies ahead.*

Torah Teacher

In 1938, R' Shraga Feivel Mendlowitz offered Rav Pam a ninth-grade position at Torah Vodaath, and he accepted the offer. He once mentioned to a talmid that when he began his career, he had asked Hashem to grant him the *zechus* (merit) to teach Torah for 60 years. The talmid shuddered as he realized that at that point, Rav Pam had already been teaching for 59 years! "Why only 60 years?" the talmid asked.

Learning in his classroom as a mesivta rebbi

Rav Pam responded with a smile. "*Zechtzig yohr iz shlecht?*" ("What's wrong with 60 years?")

Later, Rabbi Aharon Pam told that talmid: "You heard this after 59 years of teaching. To you, 60 years seemed too few. My father mentioned this to me many years ago. At that time, the thought of teaching 60 years seemed an incredible request. Who teaches for 60 years?"

Apparently, from the time he entered the classroom at age 26, Rav Pam was determined to devote his life to his talmidim, and therefore he saw 60 years of teaching as a reasonable request.

Marriage

In 1943, Rav Pam married Sarah Balmuth, who greatly valued his yearning to devote his life to teaching the word of Hashem. When the match was suggested, Rav Pam's future father-in-law, R' Chaim Aryeh ("Chaim Leib") Balmuth, mentioned it to his neighbor, Rabbi Yitzchak Hutner, legendary Rosh Yeshivah of Mesivta Rabbeinu Chaim Berlin. Rav Hutner praised Rav Pam and advised that the match be pursued.

Rabbi Yitzchak Hutner

Rav Pam's father-in-law was a talmid chacham and had learned in a kollel in Reisha, Poland, before emigrating to

R' Chaim Leib Balmuth with his grandsons (l to r): Dovid, Asher and Aharon Pam

America. R' Chaim Leib was among the very few laymen in America who owned Talmudic works such as *Chiddushei HaRashba* and *Shitah Mekubetzes* — and he made good use of them.

In America, he was among the founders of the famed "*Rayim Ahuvim* (Beloved Friends) Shul" in Brooklyn's Brownsville neighborhood. The founders were all talmidei chachamim who labored for a living by day and spent hours at night and in the early morning immersed in Torah study. After R' Chaim Leib and his family moved to East Flatbush, he would walk for over an hour on Shabbos morning to daven at *Rayim Ahuvim*.

R' Chaim Leib's wife passed away suddenly at a young age, leaving him with four daughters to raise. Despite the difficulties, his devotion to learning never waned, and this greatly influenced his daughters. When the girls would go to their rooms at night, they could hear their father learning aloud in the kitchen. When, in the course of his learning, R' Chaim Leib came across a story or aggadic teaching, he would call out, "Listen to this!" — and he would relate the thought to his daughters.

A Time to Speak Up

Even as a young man, Rav Pam commanded enormous respect. His children recall from their youth that many adults, some of them considerably older than their father, would approach him for guidance in halachah and other matters.

In his autobiography, *Lieutenant Birnbaum*, R' Meyer Birnbaum writes:

Learning with a neighbor in his study

Another great talmid chacham with whom we had frequent contact was Rabbi Avraham Pam, Rosh Yeshivah of Torah Vodaath ... Though he steadfastly refused any official position or title, he was our unofficial rav (at the Young Israel of New Lots) for a number of years.

Mr. Birnbaum recalls:

The Shechinah (Divine Presence) seemed to rest upon him. He never lectured to us, but there was one occasion when he actually came forward on his own to address us.

It was Simchas Torah. The young energetic members of the shul, most of them college students who had been educated in public schools, danced with the sefer Torah with great exuberance, even taking it out into the street and blocking traffic as they rejoiced.

The boys of the shul, most of them students of the newly founded Yeshivah Toras Chaim, were not included in the circle formed by these young men, and they made a circle of their own, without a sefer Torah, in a different part of the shul. When the young men returned from their dancing in the street, Rav Pam, uncharacteristically, tapped on the bimah as a signal for silence and in his softspoken way, addressed the minyan:

"Please excuse me, but I would like to say something. As you all know, at a wedding, the mechutanim (parents of the bride and groom) are the ones who dance in the middle with the chasan. Occasionally, they will pull in an uncle or some other relative to dance as well, while the friends who have been invited to the simchah dance in the outer circle.

"Today is Simchas Torah. Who are the real 'mechutanim' (main celebrants) at today's simchah? It is the children, those who spend a good part of their day learning Chumash with Rashi, Mishnayos or Gemara. They should be in the center circle, dancing with the Torah. Now, everyone here should make a commitment that in the coming year, he is going to dedicate time every day to the study of Torah. That way, when next Simchas Torah arrives, he too will be a 'mechutan.'"

Everyone was touched by Rav Pam's words. The dancing resumed, with the children in the center circle.

The late Mirrer Rosh Yeshivah, Rabbi Shraga Moshe Kalmanowitz, arrived in America in 1941. Often, he would visit Mesivta Torah Vodaath to discuss Torah with the Rosh Yeshivah, Rabbi Shlomo Heiman. Once, R' Shlomo told Rabbi Kalmanowitz regarding Rav Pam: *"Unter dem yunger man, vakst an adam gadol* (Beneath this [seemingly ordinary] young man, a great Torah personality is developing)." Rav Pam was then around 30 years old.

Seemingly Ordinary

Rav Pam's children recall that as they were growing up, they did not see their father as an outstanding personality. He did everything in a calm, softspoken manner without fanfare, and it never occurred to them that they were witnessing something special. Only after they matured did they begin to realize that their father was a man of rare qualities.

When they were young, there were no fans in the house, as a safety precaution. Air conditioning was an unheard-of luxury, so when the hot, humid summer days arrived, there was nothing to do but sweat. There was a small room which faced the sun

Rabbi Shraga Moshe Kalmanowitz greeting Rav Pam. At left is Rabbi Elya Svei.

in the afternoon and which served as Rav Pam's study. His children recall that on the hottest summer days, he would sit in that room for hours on end, deeply immersed in his learning.

When their apartment was being painted, Rav Pam learned in the kitchen and was able to immerse himself in his studies as always, despite whatever was going on around him.

Lessons in Honesty

Rav Pam was known for his passion for truth in both speech and action. His children learned this at a young age.

Once, he took them on a city bus and handed the driver fare for everyone. The driver attempted to return one fare. "He rides for free," the driver said, motioning to the youngest boy who appeared to be under age. "No, he *is* of age," Rav Pam replied, and he paid the fare.

On another occasion, Rav Pam and his oldest son, Aharon, entered a taxi. After about a minute, Aharon realized that the meter was not running, and he pointed this out to his father. Rav Pam mentioned this to the driver and was stunned by his reply: "Rabbi, this ride is for me!" — meaning that he was purposely not running the meter so that he could pocket the entire fare instead of handing over a percentage to the taxi company. Rav Pam insisted that the meter be turned on and assured the driver that he would satisfy him. True to his word, he gave the man a very generous tip which left him happy. To Rav Pam, the importance of being honest far outweighed the extra money he had spent.

Some years later, Rav Pam and his youngest son, Asher, were on their way to yeshivah on a frigid Sunday morning. They were running late and the walk to the subway would take about 15 minutes. When a lone taxi came down the street, Rav Pam flagged it down and asked that they be driven to the subway station.

They soon realized that the meter was not running. When Rav Pam asked the driver about this, he replied, "Rabbi, I'm driving around for an hour looking for business. I *can't afford* to start the meter and report this trip!"

"Please," Rav Pam pleaded, "start the meter. I cannot travel with you if you don't." The driver, however, refused to cooperate.

"If you don't turn on the meter," Rav Pam said, "I will have to leave the taxi."

"You can't do that, Rabbi," the driver countered, "it's freezing outside." And he continued to drive with the meter off.

At the next corner, Rav Pam said, "Please stop; I'm getting off here." He paid what would have been the full fare to the subway station, added a tip, and left the cab along with his son. As they walked to the subway, Asher asked his father why he had paid the man so much. "To make sure that he would not feel we wronged him," Rav Pam replied.

Other Lessons

The Pam children learned many other lessons as well. One day, the family waited on an elevated train platform for the next train. Nearby stood a gentile woman and her little boy. A wind came along and blew the boy's hat onto the tracks. There were no curves in the tracks for at least two stations. Rav Pam peered down the tracks and, seeing no trains in the distance, he climbed down and retrieved the hat. (Meanwhile, Rebbetzin Pam showed her young sons that their father was carefully avoiding the third rail, through which electricity flows.) After climbing back up and returning the hat to the grateful boy and his mother, Rav Pam cautioned his children that until they grew up, they must never do what he did.

When the oldest child, Aharon, was an infant, the family rented a room on a farm in upstate New York for a few weeks during the summer. As Rebbetzin Pam recalls, Rav Pam did not sleep very much during those weeks. There were other families on the premises and the thin cottage walls did not block out sounds very well. So during the night, Rav or Rebbetzin Pam would take the baby out of his crib as soon as he began to cry, so as not to disturb anyone's sleep.

Consideration for the needs and feelings of others was a way of life in the Pam home. When the Pam children were very young, the family lived in a three-room apartment; it had a parents' bedroom, a children's bedroom and a kitchen. One of their neighbors was a bachelor who enjoyed doing word puzzles, but he sometimes had difficulty figuring out the clues. When he knocked on the Pams' door for help, he was graciously received. The man would spread his puzzle sheets on the kitchen table and whenever he got stuck on a clue, Rav Pam would help him.

It happened once that Rav Pam found a $5 bill in the street, which was a significant sum in those days. The money sat on a dresser for a few days, until Rav Pam gave it to *tzedakah*. He explained to the children that whoever had lost the money had surely suffered distress over it. How could one benefit from money that came to him through someone else's pain?

CHAPTER FOUR

Love of Torah and Its Students

Rav Pam was delivering a *shiur* to his beis midrash talmidim. When he reached the conclusion of a very beautiful and important *pshat* (explanation), he exclaimed, "For such a *pshat*, we should make a *kiddush*!" Rav Pam was not suggesting that they actually celebrate with a *kiddush*. But as a person who was unusually careful with his words, he meant what he said. To him, an explanation in Gemara that shed new light on the topic was so meaningful, so exciting, that it was reason enough to celebrate. Such

Sharing his Torah thoughts with others.

was Rav Pam's love for every bit of Torah knowledge.

As a young talmid in Yeshivah Torah Vodaath, Rav Pam's son, R' Asher, would travel to yeshivah each morning together with his father. The subway station was a fifteen-minute walk from their home. On cold days, Rav Pam was reluctant to talk with his son as they walked because he found that this strained his voice. Asher would hear his father whispering to himself, "So the *Rashba* is saying," as he verbalized the Gemara that he was reviewing in his mind.

Once, a talmid on his way to yeshivah met Rav Pam waiting for a bus to take him to Mesivta Rabbeinu Chaim Berlin, where a meeting of roshei yeshivah was to take place. When the talmid offered to get his car and drive Rav Pam there, he replied,

"*Chas v'shalom* that I should disturb a *bachur's* learning."

One day, Rav Pam left yeshivah as it began to rain. A talmid ran out to hold an umbrella over him. Rav Pam said, "The hat is an old hat, the coat is an old coat, the Jew is an old Jew — better that you go back inside and learn!"

Engrossed in thought on his way to yeshivah

On Simchas Torah 5760 (1999), Rav Pam addressed the minyan in his home after *hakafos*. He related the story of a group of concentration camp prisoners who were sent to the gas chambers on Simchas Torah. Well aware of the fate that awaited them, they joined hands and danced joyously in honor of the Torah. Rav Pam wept as he said, "What should we, who are able to learn Torah, say? How joyous should we be...!"

Rav Shisgal

Among Rav Pam's closest friends was Rabbi Eliyahu Moshe Shisgal, who for a number of years taught the grade above Rav Pam at Mesivta Torah Vodaath. Rav Shisgal, who was the son-in-law of Rabbi Moshe Feinstein, passed away in 1973 at the age of 52. He had a lightning-quick mind and sought out every opportunity to discuss Torah with the Torah genius of the day, Rabbi Aharon Kotler. Few who observed the two discuss Torah could follow the pace of their conversation. When Rav Shisgal was in his early 30s, Rav

Rabbi Eliyahu Moshe Shisgal with his father-in-law, Rabbi Moshe Feinstein

Aharon referred to him as a "*gadol baTorah*" (great Torah personality).

On afternoons when classes were dismissed early, Rav Pam and Rav Shisgal would walk together to the Willamsburg Bridge Plaza, discussing Torah. At the Plaza they were to part — Rav Pam to continue on to the subway station and Rav Shisgal to take the bus over the bridge to the Lower East Side. However, rather than see their discussion end, they would walk one another back and forth, from Bridge Plaza to the subway station, until the advancing hour left them no choice but to head for home.

Rav Shisgal discussing Torah with Rabbi Aharon Kotler

One summer, when the Pam family rented a bungalow in the Catskill Mountains, Rav Shisgal paid Rav Pam a surprise visit. When told that Rav Pam had just gone to nap, but was not yet sleeping, Rav Shisgal pleaded, "Please do not disturb him! I will wait until he gets up — it is *k'dai* (worthwhile) to wait." He had brought with him a *Masechta Shabbos* and he proceeded to study from it for the next two hours until Rav Pam awoke.

Rav Shisgal once remarked, "I thank the *Ribono shel Olam* for Rav Pam — what would we do without him?"

When Rav Shisgal passed away, Rav Pam was overcome with grief. When he fulfilled the mitzvah of *nichum aveilim* (comforting the mourners), he asked to be shown the room in which his beloved friend had studied, a room whose walls were saturated with the *kedushah* of Torah study. Rav Pam stood silently in the room for a few minutes, and then left.

Rav Pam related that Rav Shisgal once appeared to him in a dream with such clarity that when Rav Pam awoke, he recalled the entire Torah discussion that had taken place between them in the dream.

With Reb Aharon

Rav Pam would accompany Rav Shisgal and Rav Gedaliah Schorr (who preceded Rav Pam as Rosh Yeshivah of Torah Vodaath) to Manhattan to attend an afternoon *shiur* for talmidei chachamim in *Mishnayos Pe'ah*, given by Rabbi Aharon Kotler. This was during the Second World War, soon after Reb Aharon had arrived in America and prior to his founding the great Torah fortress, Beth Medrash Govoha of Lakewood.

Greeting Reb Aharon at a wedding. Rabbi Tzadok Shaingarten is in the background.

Rav Pam related that once, he witnessed how Reb Aharon seemed to possess a supernatural power of hearing when words of Torah were spoken. When Reb Aharon delivered his Mishnayos *shiur*, he would sit at the head of a long table. Once, Rav Pam and Rav Shisgal were seated at the opposite end of the table from Reb Aharon. At one point, Rav Pam turned to Rav Shisgal and, in a whisper, commented on something Reb Aharon had just said. Reb Aharon immediately looked towards Rav Pam and responded to the comment!

Asher Pam received a rare reprimand from his father on the day following Reb Aharon's passing. It was erev Shabbos and Asher was humming a tune as he went about his Shabbos preparations. "How can you sing when Reb Aharon was just *niftar*?" his father demanded.

After the funeral, Rav Pam addressed his mesivta class. He said that Reb Aharon's passing was a tremendous loss, and it was everyone's responsibility to do his share to try to make up for that loss. He suggested to the boys that for the remainder of the school year, they should devote some of their recess to Torah study. He recommended that they undertake to study an additional *perek* (chapter) of Gemara and that they learn it *b'iyun* (in depth), for this was the kind of learning that Reb Aharon had stressed. All the boys agreed to this, and for the rest of the year during the half-hour break between Torah and secular studies, Rav Pam taught the class the sixth *perek* of *Masechta Bava Kamma.*

The Greatest Joy

As mentioned, when Rav Pam turned 80, Mesivta Torah Vodaath launched a campaign to write a *sefer Torah* in his honor. At a reception held to initiate the campaign, Rav Pam said:

> *The blessing of life is what you do with it. I am grateful beyond words to HaKadosh Baruch Hu that He has led me to Yeshivah Torah Vodaath and to be associated with talmidim...*
>
> *I'm with the yeshivah's talmidim every day, and one might think that you take things for granted when you experience the same thing day after day. But my excitement, my joy at this association with the talmidim, is as fresh as the day it started ...*
>
> *As grateful as I am to HaKadosh Baruch Hu for the 80 years of life that He has given me, I am even more grateful for the 56 years [thus far] of teaching talmidim ...*

Celebrating with his talmidim on Purim 5724 (1964)

A talmid recalled:

> *Sitting in the beis midrash of Mesivta Torah Vodaath some 20 years ago, I was faced with a major dilemma. Should I continue along the path that would lead to a career in business and accounting, or enter the world of chinuch (Torah education)?*
>
> *Rav Pam told me: "Some people will tell you to enter chinuch because this way your [portion in] Olam Haba (the World to Come) will be assured. And I tell you that you should enter the world of chinuch because there is no greater simchah in* ***this*** *world than to teach Torah to Jewish children."*
>
> *In my mind's eye, I can still see Rav Pam's radiant smile as he uttered these words.*

Polishing Diamonds

In 1975, Rav Pam was honored by Mesivta Torah Vodaath, at a dinner held in the Mesivta dining room. In his address, he related a *mashal* of the Chofetz Chaim:

> *A diamond merchant traveled for weeks by coach to reach the location of a special market. Someone was selling a beautiful diamond, which the merchant knew he could resell at a handsome*

profit, but the asking price was more than he had with him.

After a week, when the market was about to close, that special diamond was still not sold. The merchant offered the seller all the money he had, except his fare home. But the seller would agree to the deal only if the merchant also included that money. The merchant made the deal, even though he knew that it would take him months to walk home in the cold winter.

He took the diamond, wrapped it in cloth and started trudging his way home.

Addressing a gathering in the dining room of Mesivta Torah Vodaath

There were nights when he almost froze to death. In desperation, he took out the diamond, planning to sell it at any price to whoever would buy it. However, as soon as he unwrapped the beautiful, sparkling gem and was reminded of its beauty and value, he was filled with new spirit.

When he finally arrived home, his family asked him, "How did you overcome the difficulties of the journey back?" He answered that each time he was ready to give up, the glow of the diamond gave him the strength to continue.

Rav Pam concluded: Teaching Torah is not always easy. However, the knowledge that one is devoting his time and talents to producing "diamonds" — the *bnei Torah* of the new generation — gives one the strength and spirit to go on.

The Best Remedy

In the fall of 1991, Rav Pam developed high blood pressure and other medical problems. He was hospitalized for tests; after being discharged, he returned to yeshivah but still was not feeling well. At the conclusion of *shiur* one day, he announced that the next week and a half would be devoted to review and that he would not deliver *shiurim* during this period, though he would be in yeshivah to "speak in learning" with his talmidim.

Poring over a sugya with Rabbi Reuven Scheiner

A few older talmidim approached him and suggested that he go to a resort to rest for ten days, but Rav Pam would not agree. The talmidim then suggested that their rebbi rest at home for ten days. They offered to organize daily *minyanim* in his home and suggested that a specific time of day be designated for the talmidim to come and discuss their learning with him. Rav Pam did not accept these suggestions. Rav Pam's grandson explained to a talmid, "More than anything, my grandfather is pained by the fact that his illness forced him to miss being in yeshivah. To suggest that he stay home for ten days or go away on vacation would make him worse."

Shortly thereafter, a renowned rav suggested that Rav Pam take a vacation. Rav Pam replied that there was no better remedy for him than to be in yeshivah with his talmidim.

Rav Pam's Weekly Shmuessen

For decades, Rav Pam delivered a *shmuess* (*mussar* lecture) in a classroom or small beis midrash on Erev Shabbos. From the time that he became Rosh Yeshivah of Torah Vodaath (in the early 1980s), he delivered a *shmuess* in the main beis midrash for all talmidim on the Thursday before Shabbos *Mevarchim*.

His shmuessen became classics in the Torah world. Rabbi Chaim Ozer Grodzensky once compared the Chofetz Chaim's words to the *mann* in the Midbar; just as the *mann* was enjoyed on various levels and tasted different to different people, so too the Chofetz

Chaim's holy words were appreciated by each person on his or her level.

The same can be said of Rav Pam's words. Distinguished rabbis, kollel members and younger students all heard the same shmuess from Rav Pam and everyone walked away with his own personal, important message.

There were talmidim who attended Rav Pam's shmuessen for over *20 years*. Even when they heard the same shmuess a second or third time, they felt enriched and uplifted.

Rav Pam kisses the paroches before addressing talmidim in the Torah Vodaath beis midrash

In the final year of Rav Pam's life, poor health forced him to sit while delivering his weekly shmuess. Men from all walks of life would join talmidim of Torah Vodaath to drink from Rav Pam's wisdom.

A certain talmid eventually left Torah Vodaath and went to study in America's Mirrer Yeshivah. He would return to Torah Vodaath each week with a tape recorder and notebook, so that he could record his rebbi's shmuess on tape and on paper. One week, on the Thursday before Shabbos *Mevarchim,* he arrived late. As he hurried into the beis midrash, Rav Pam was already ascending the podium to begin speaking. The talmid felt that it would not be respectful to walk up to the front of the beis midrash to set up his tape recorder. He sat down in a seat in the back row of the beis midrash and took out his notebook. However, Rav Pam noticed him, and motioned for him to come forward with his tape recorder. The talmid obeyed. Rav Pam did not begin speaking until his talmid was seated.

A Higher Standard

There was an underlying message in Rav Pam's shmuessen which everyone understood, and which Rav Pam's talmidim strive to live by: A *ben Torah* must see himself as an "ambassador" of Torah, and always ensure that his words and actions bring honor to Hashem's Name.

Rav Pam was fond of recounting a well-known parable of the Dubno Maggid:

> *A wealthy man was seeking a husband for his only daughter. He traveled to a renowned yeshivah and told the rosh yeshivah that he was seeking an outstanding talmid chacham whom he was prepared to support for years to come. The Rosh Yeshivah said, "I have just the right young man for you. He has the best mind of any of my students and he is also the most diligent among them, spending days and night in study without interruption."*
>
> *The wedding took place and the new couple moved into the father-in-law's home, as was the custom. However, the father-in-law was dismayed when he discovered that his son-in-law was spending only an hour or two studying each day! When the young man was confronted he responded, "Why should I study more? The people in this city are basically ignorant. If I were to stop learning entirely, and even if I forgot some of what I've already learned, I would still be the greatest talmid chacham in town!"*
>
> *"Your outlook is all wrong," his father-in-law replied sadly. "Your goal should not be to outdo your fellow townspeople. You have to be the best that you can possibly be, which is to stand out even among an exceptional group of scholars, as you did when you were learning in yeshivah."*

Said Rav Pam: A *ben Torah* cannot be satisfied that his *midos* are superior to what is found in the secular world. The fact that he is a *ben Torah*, a product of yeshivos, who has made Torah study his primary focus, requires that he live up to a higher standard in all areas. Nothing less than excellence will do.

In the beis midrash kattan of Mesivta Torah Vodaath. Rabbi Moshe Wolfson is seated at right.

"Minor" Details

Rav Pam would remind his talmidim of seemingly "minor" items that he considered quite important. Rav Pam considered them important because he recognized that a *ben Torah's* every word and deed must proclaim that the Torah's ways are "ways of pleasantness" (*Mishlei* 4:2).

Before *bein hazemanim* (intercession), he would urge his talmidim to be helpful at home, to be available for shopping,

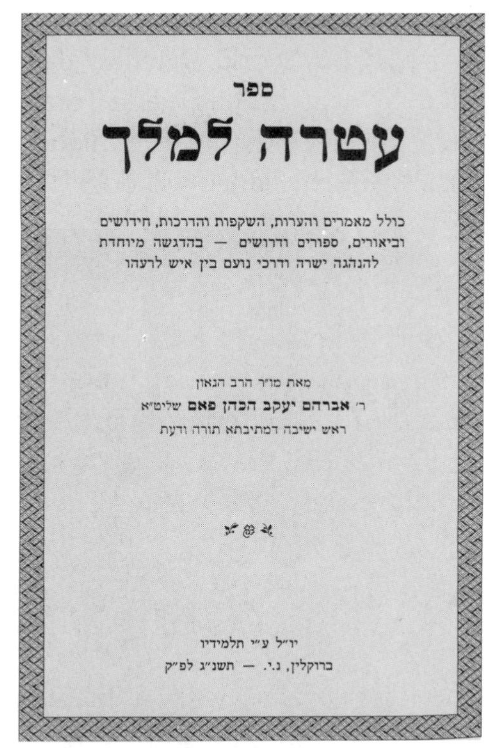
ספר

עטרה למלך

כולל מאמרים והערות, השקפות והדרכות, חידושים
וביאורים, ספורים ודרושים — בהדגשה מיוחדת
להנהגה ישרה ודרכי נועם בין איש לרעהו

מאת מו״ר הרב הגאון
ר׳ **אברהם יעקב הכהן פאם** שליט״א
ראש ישיבה דמתיבתא תורה ודעת

יו״ל ע״י תלמידיו
ברוקלין, נ.י. — תשנ״ג לפ״ק

In the year 5753 (1993), a collection of Rav Pam's shmuessen were published in Hebrew. In the introduction to the sefer, entitled Atarah LaMelech (A Crown for the King), Rav Pam wrote that when a ben Torah is crowned with the crown of good midos, he glorifies the Name of Hashem.

and to be prepared to offer *divrei Torah* (Torah thoughts) at the Shabbos and Yom Tov meals.

In his final shmuess before the summer recess, he would speak of how a *ben Torah* should conduct himself during his vacation. Of course, he expected his talmidim to maintain fixed sessions in Torah study and to always daven with a *minyan*. But he expected more. "If you are going to camp, make sure that you do not make fun of the food." He would go on to describe how hard a camp cook works and the pain that he or she is liable to suffer if the food is ridiculed. And he would remind them to thank the cook for his or her efforts.

He would add some advice for those who were exceptionally dedicated to their studies. "If learning 15 extra minutes will mean coming late to lunch and causing the waiter to work harder, it's not worth it."

A Rule to Live By

Once, as the term was nearing its end, a student in Rav Pam's mesivta class, who lived in South America, raised his hand and said, "I am returning home to my family, and when I meet my non-religious aunts, they will offer their hands in greeting. What should I do?"

Rav Pam responded, "For a long time now, I have lived by the following rule: If one behaves in a pleasant, refined manner, then people will respect him though he is different than they are. Tell your aunts in a respectful manner that as a yeshivah student, your way is to avoid shaking hands with women."

Like Sons

At a wedding, Rav Pam was talking with a talmid. Someone passing by asked, "Is that your son?" "Yes," Rav Pam replied, "like a son."

Dancing with a talmid at his wedding

A talmid from the 1960s related: "I was not the typical 'Torah Vodaath boy,' and I was not what you would call a '*masmid*' (diligent student). Rav Pam arranged for a beis midrash student to learn with me every day. Years later I discovered that Rav Pam had paid this fellow to learn with me — *from his own money*! In a sense, I've been trying to 'pay him back' ever since."

He was an accomplished mathematician. Once, one of his talmidim was not learning well because he was preoccupied with a math exam, a subject in which he was weak. Rav Pam made a deal with him. "You concentrate on the Gemara and I will tutor you for the test."

A talmid's son related an episode which probably was repeated many times:

> *In the summer of 1987, we celebrated my younger brother's bar mitzvah. Rav Pam had not been feeling well, so my father sent him an invitation (out of respect and closeness), but did not call to ask if he would come. My father did not want his rebbi to strain himself to attend and he was afraid that if he would call, Rav Pam would feel an obligation to attend. My father assumed that if he did not call, the Rosh Yeshivah would not come.*
>
> *In the middle of the bar mitzvah, Rav Pam walked in! I hurried over to him and sat him at the head table. My father, looking quite embarrassed, apologized for not sending a car to bring his rebbi to the simchah. He then began to apologize for not calling to ask if Rav Pam would attend. Rav Pam stopped him in mid-sentence. "There was no need*

to call and there was certainly no need to make arrangements for me. I received an invitation from my talmid, I made note of it, and I came."

"My Greatest Pleasure"

A young woman who was expecting a baby was told by her doctor that she should be prepared to give birth to a very sick child. The woman and her husband were, understandably, very distressed. Her husband immediately called his rebbi, Rav Pam. This was a year before Rav Pam

Rav Pam was Rabbi Nachum Gold's rebbi in 1951. Rebbi and talmid remained close until Rav Pam's passing 50 years later. In this photograph, Rav Pam is dancing with Rabbi Gold at the wedding of the latter's daughter. In circle (counterclockwise from upper right): Rabbi Moshe Dovid Steinwurzel and יבל"ח Rabbi Tzvi Yehudah Basch, Rabbi Lipa Margulies and Rabbi Shlomo Feivel Schustal.

passed away. Though he was very ill, he told his talmid to come to his house along with his wife.

Rav Pam offered the couple much *chizuk* (emotional support) and a warm *berachah*. His words had a calming effect on the wife, and she greatly appreciated that Rav Pam, in his ill and weakened state, had given them so much of his precious time. Before leaving, she said, "I have a request to make. *B'ezras Hashem*, if it will be a boy, would the Rosh Yeshivah honor us by being *sandak*?"

Rav Pam probably recalled that he had already been *sandak* for the couple's first son. Rav Pam followed the common custom (that of the *Maharil*) not to serve as *sandak* for more than one son in a family. However, in this case, he made an exception. "It would be my greatest pleasure to be *sandak*," he replied warmly.

A few months later, the woman gave birth to a healthy baby boy. The husband phoned Rav Pam's son, R' Aharon, to tell him the news and to inform him of what Rav Pam had said some months earlier. R' Aharon replied that his father had just returned

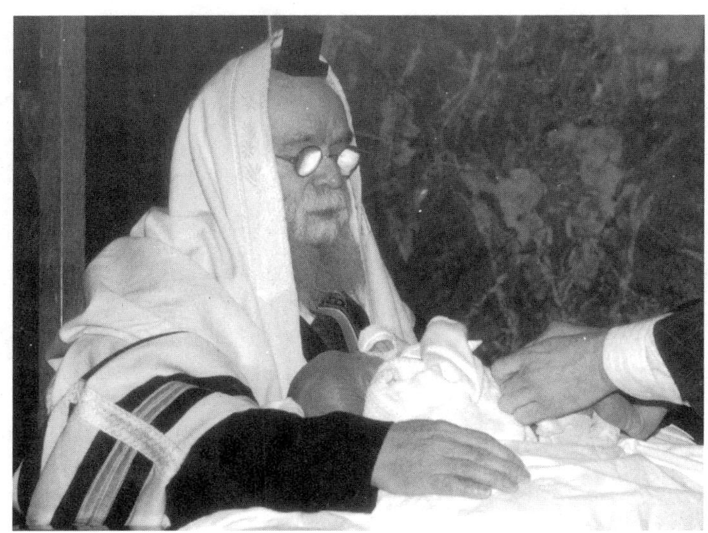

As sandak

home from a stay in the hospital and the family would have to wait a couple of days to see if he could accept the honor of *sandak*.

Later that week, the couple received a phone call from Rav Pam's family — he would be able to serve as *sandak*. When Rav Pam took the phone, his talmid said, "While we would be so honored to have Rebbi be *sandak*, we fully understand if it is too difficult."

"It would be my greatest pleasure," Rav Pam replied softly.

It was decided to arrange the bris in a way that would minimize the strain for Rav Pam as much as possible. Davening and the bris took place in Rav Pam's home. Only a minyan of men and a couple of women were present. After the bris, cake and schnapps were served, a "L'Chaim!" was made, and then a *seudas mitzvah* was held elsewhere to which many guests had been invited.

Like Grandchildren

Rav Pam's love for his talmidim's children was like that of a grandfather for his grandchildren.

Once, a talmid brought his family for a visit at a time when Rebbetzin Pam was not home. Rav Pam took some cookies out of the freezer and defrosted them in the toaster oven for the children. When one of the children seemed particularly fond of a toy car, Rav Pam picked it up, handed it to the child and said, "Here, this is a present for you."

A talmid once said to him, "I just want to thank Rebbi for all that he has done for me." Rav Pam smiled and replied, "It's really my pleasure. If boys learn and understand learning and continue learning after they have left yeshivah — that is the biggest 'Thank you.' "

For Every Ben Torah

Rebbeim, especially former talmidim, would often bring their talmidim to Rav Pam. Rav Pam always greeted the boys with love and would use the opportunity to instill in them a love of Torah.

A former talmid who was a ninth-grade rebbi would bring his class to Rav Pam at the conclusion of the school year, when the class would complete a small *masechta*. The *siyum* was held in Rav Pam's home; Rebbetzin Pam would bake a cake in honor of the occasion.

> *Besides discussing their learning with them, Rav Pam would inspire the boys with thoughts on the greatness of Torah study. "You enjoy drinking this soda," he once said, as he pointed to a bottle on the table. "Well, that pleasure does not compare to the pleasure of someone who is walking in the hot sun and quenches his thirst with some cold water. As Shlomo HaMelech said, 'Like cold water on a weary soul' (Mishlei 25:25). Torah is likened to water — no pleasure can compare to it!"*

Another rebbi would bring his talmidim to receive Rav Pam's *berachah* after they had completed a *masechta*. Once, when the rebbi apologized for having bothered Rav Pam and taken of his time, Rav Pam replied, "Bother? I *enjoy* giving *berachos* to *bnei Torah*!"

After receiving the Rosh Yeshivah's *berachah,* each talmid was photographed individually with him. One year, one photograph did not come out. The rebbi asked Rav Pam if the picture could be retaken. Rav Pam sat at his desk in his office

Greeting young bnei Torah.

and the talmid, who was quite tall, stood next to him. Before the picture was snapped, Rav Pam said, "I don't think the picture will come out good." He had the boy sit down next to him and asked that a light be turned on to give better lighting. Sensing that the boy was uncomfortable sitting next to him behind his desk, Rav Pam put his arm around him, and then the picture was taken.

Learn with Joy

Rav Pam would say that serving Hashem with joy is the key to growth as a G-d-fearing Jew and *ben Torah.* Joy is a key ingredient in learning Torah; the Mishnah (*Avos* 6:6) lists *"simchah"* as one of the 48 ways in which Torah is acquired.

Once, he was asked to speak with a student who had little interest in learning and was floundering in yeshivah. In his

Imparting the joy of Torah learning to talmidim of Yeshivah Darchei Torah

warm, caring way, Rav Pam told him, "I'm asking you a favor: not that you should learn a lot, but that whatever you learn, you should learn with *simchah,* because then it goes into your bloodstream and never goes out.

"Remember: It was worth it for Hashem to create the entire world just for a few minutes of your learning."

In his last years, Rav Pam was visited by an eighth-grade yeshivah student whom he had never met. The boy excelled in his learning and could not decide which mesivta to attend in the coming school year. He had been accepted into an excellent, established mesivta, but he was being urged to enroll in a new mesivta that had earned itself a good reputation in a short amount of time. This school was eager to have this boy as a talmid; and once his enrollment became known, other such boys would likely enroll as well.

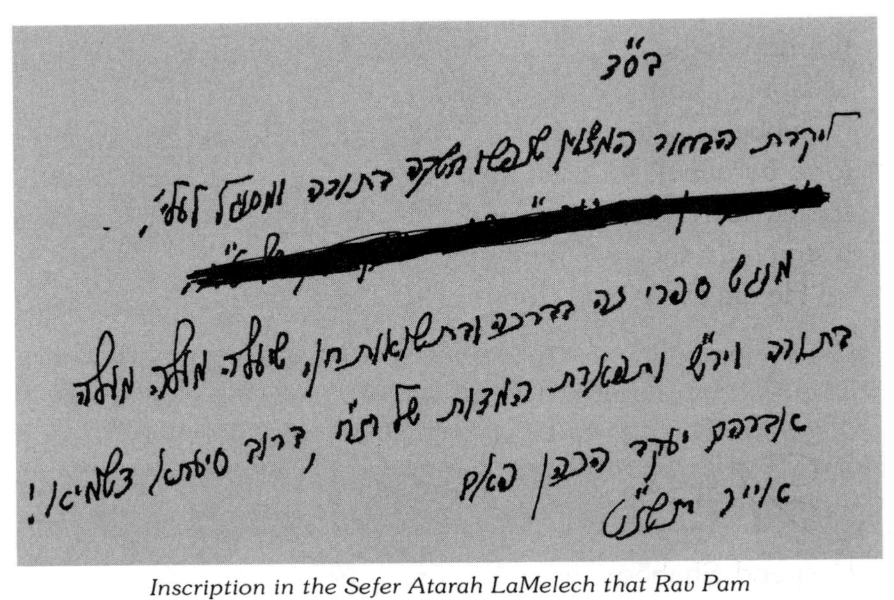

Inscription in the Sefer Atarah LaMelech that Rav Pam gave to the eighth-grade student

In their first meeting, Rav Pam asked the boy, "In which mesivta do you think you will learn with more *simchah*?" The boy named the established mesivta. Initially, Rav Pam said to choose that mesivta, but after another session with the boy, he decided in favor of the other school. "It is a great *zechus* to have a share in building a *makom* (place of) Torah," he told the boy. "But you must learn *b'simchah*," he stressed, "and of course, your father must make the final decision. Your *chinuch* (Torah education) is his responsibility."

He then took out a new copy of his *Sefer Atarah LaMelech* and sat down to learn with the boy. They studied some insights regarding the importance of studying Torah with joy. When they were finished, Rav Pam inscribed the *sefer* and presented it to the boy as a gift. Before the boy left, Rav Pam told him, "I want you to call me every so often and let me know how you are doing. And if you do go to the new mesivta and you are not happy there, I will do everything in my power to have you accepted into the other mesivta."

Rebbetzin Pam recalls: "When people would ask Rav Pam for a *berachah* for their sons, he would *bentch* them that they should learn *b'simchah*; and he would say that if they learn *b'simchah*, they will remember what they learn.

"He did everything *b'simchah*; he was a very happy person."

Lending a Hand

A teenager was having a difficult time in mesivta and was on a downward turn. His rebbi arranged for him to spend Shabbos in Kensington where an older boy was to bring him to Rav Pam's minyan. The rebbi spoke to Rav Pam in advance of the boy's visit. After *Minchah*, as the members of the minyan filed out, Rav Pam took hold of the boy's hand and said, "I'd like you to join us for *Shalosh Seudos*."

Rav Pam sat the boy next to him. For a long time, he held the boy's hand as Shabbos *zemiros* were sung. That night after

Attending an eighth-grade siyum at Yeshivah Torah Vodaath.

Havdalah, the boy phoned his parents and said, "I don't want to ever wash my hand — Rav Pam held it for 15 minutes!"

Some time later, the boy and his mother visited Rav Pam together. The mother wanted her son to take life more seriously and so she asked Rav Pam, "What does the Rosh Yeshivah think of 'fun'?"

Rav Pam understood what she wanted, but first he wanted the boy to realize that an older rosh yeshivah was once a teenager, and understood a young person's needs.

"Fun?" Rav Pam responded, his eyes lighting up. "When we were young, oh, did we have fun! We played ball ..."

Largely thanks to Rav Pam's influence, the boy's learning improved and he began to change in other ways as well. Today, he is a fine *ben Torah* and brings much *nachas* to his parents.

A man who had been involved in helping many yeshivos and rebbeim brought his grandsons to Rav Pam for a *berachah*. Rav Pam said to them. "I'm going to give you the best *berachah* I have — that all of you should become *marbitzei Torah* (those who spread Torah). Could there be a better *berachah*?"

CHAPTER FIVE

Leader of the Generation

For most of his life, Rav Pam was not involved in public affairs; his focus was on the study and teaching of Torah. His schedule was a very organized one.

In his later years when he taught the *Yoreh De'ah shiur* in Torah Vodaath, Rav Pam spent the morning at home learning and was in yeshivah in the afternoon to deliver his *shiur* and be available to his talmidim. His nights were often devoted to conversations with former talmidim who would either call or come in person to benefit from his sage advice. And he devoted time to preparing

Rabbi Gedaliah Schorr

and delivering his weekly "alumni *shiur*" for former talmidim, which was very important to him.

His life changed drastically in 1979 when the Rosh Yeshivah of Torah Vodaath, Rabbi Gedaliah Schorr, passed away suddenly. For the next two years, the yeshivah was led by a *vaad* (committee) which included Rav Pam. Two years later, Rav Pam was recognized as Rosh Yeshivah.

At around the same time, something else caused a major change in Rav Pam's life. In happened in 1982. One day, Rav Pam told a talmid, "R' Yaakov [Kamenetsky] hung up on me!" He explained, "I was invited to join the *Moetzes Gedolei HaTorah,*[1] but declined. R' Yaakov then called and told me that he felt I should not refuse. As I began to explain why I felt that I could not agree, I heard a click on the other side. [R' Yaakov had hung up the phone.] R' Yaakov was not giving me a choice."

R' Yaakov, as well as other *gedolim*, had decided that the time had come for Rav Pam to take a more active role in leading the generation.

Rav Pam did not want the position because it would cut into the precious time he devoted to guiding his talmidim and to his own personal learning. And, in his deep humility, he considered himself unworthy of being part of a group that included Rav Moshe Feinstein, Rav Yaakov Kamenetsky and other *gedolei Yisrael*.

1. Council of Torah Sages of Agudath Israel.

With Rabbi Yaakov Kamenetsky

That same year, he was asked, for the first time, to spend Shabbos at the annual Agudath Israel convention. He reluctantly agreed. When someone asked why he did not decline the invitation, Rav Pam replied, "What? And trouble R' Yaakov to call me *again*?"

Addressing an Agudath Israel convention. Rabbi Moshe Sherer is at left.

The Philadelphia Rosh Yeshivah, Rabbi Elya Svei, was a fellow *Moetzes* member. After Rav Pam's passing, he said, "Though I did not learn under him, I consider myself his talmid. There was never a meeting that we both attended where I did not learn something from him."

The Will of Hashem

Rav Pam once said with a smile, "My Rebbetzin has complaints against me. She says, 'Why did I marry you? Because you were sitting and learning. Now you are busy going to meetings and making speeches. You don't learn!' "

Another time he remarked, "My dream was that I would retire as my father did, and I would be able to learn all day and night. *Ah* ... look what has become of me! The community needs have been thrust upon me. I had wanted so badly to learn ..."

But Rav Pam accepted his new role as the will of Hashem. He once told his rebbetzin, "Why do I sit and learn? Because that is what the *Ribono shel Olam* wants us to do. Apparently, the *Ribono shel Olam* now wants me to become involved in *tzorchei tzibbur* (communal matters). And if that is what the *Ribono shel Olam* wants, that is what I have to do."

In his later years, Rav Pam accepted a much more difficult change in his life as the will of Hashem. In 1997, when major surgery was followed by frequent, difficult treatments, he was initially upset at how this was affecting his daily schedule of learning and teaching. However, Rav Pam then adjusted to the situation. As a result, he directed much of his time and energy to *chesed*, which he was able to accomplish from his home when he was confined there much of the time because of poor health.

Rav Pam in his final years

At that time, he explained: He no longer had the strength for long, intensive periods of study, and often, he could not attend minyan. He decided that it was Hashem's will at that point in time that he become involved in assisting individuals and organizations with personal letters, phone calls and even meetings in his home to raise funds. From then until the end of Rav Pam's life, millions of dollars in tzedakah funds were raised through his personal involvement.

Rabbi Sherer

For many years, Rabbi Moshe Sherer served as President of Agudath Israel of America. He was a devoted spokesman for *Klal Yisrael* and a loyal emissary of *gedolei Yisrael.*

With Rabbi Moshe Sherer

Rabbi Sherer often consulted Rav Pam on important issues, and the two enjoyed a very close and special relationship. During Rabbi Sherer's final illness, he received a letter from Rav Pam which, he said, was among the most precious he had received in his long career. In it, Rav Pam wrote:

This past Shabbos before Mussaf, when we recited in the Mi Shebeirach prayer, "...and all those who are involved faithfully with the needs of the community — may HaKadosh Baruch Hu pay their reward and remove from them every suffering, heal their entire body ..." I thought to myself, "Ribono shel Olam, to whom can these words of blessing refer more than Your faithful servant, Moshe ben Basya Bluma? Is there any more faithful activist for our community than he?"

... I once heard from Rabbi Chaim Kreiswirth[2] *that Talmud Yerushalmi states: "The blessing of one who loves you should not be insignificant in your eyes." Therefore, I send you this blessing from the depths of my heart ...*

---

2. The late Rav of Antwerp. Rabbi Kreiswirth, a renowned *gaon*, once told an acquaintance that he looked forward to "speaking in learning" with Rav Pam on his visits to the United States.

אברהם פאם
RABBI ABRAHAM PAM
582 EAST SEVENTH STREET
BROOKLYN, NEW YORK 11218

בס"ד יום ג' לס' "אני ה' רופאך", תשנ"ח

כבוד ידיד נפשי הרב ר' משה שערער שליט"א - שלו' רב לאוהבי'!
ביום שבת שעבר לפני מוסף, כשהתפללנו תפלת "מי שברך" וכל מי שעוסקים
בצרכי צבור באמונה הקב"ה ישלם שכרם ויסיר מהם כל מחלה וירפא לכל גופם וכו',
אמרתי בלבי: רבש"ע, למי הדברים מכוונים ומתאימים יותר מאשר בנוגע, מאשר
[illegible] ידידי הרוממו, כלום יש לך עוסק בצרכי צבור באמונה יותר ממנו?
ולכן, אמינא ואמרי כל ישראל נשואות אליך, שתסיר ממנו כל מחלה ותשלח לו
רפו"ש מן השמים במהרה בתוך שאר חולי ישראל... עד כאן רחשי לבי ותפלתי בלחש
ביום ש"ק.
שמעתי בשם הגאון מוה"ר חיים קרייזווירט שליט"א, שיש לשון [illegible]:
"אל תהי ברכת הדיוט קלה בעיניך". ולכן, הנני שולח לך ברכתי מעומקא דלבאי
שתזכה השלמה. לבוא ולשמחך ברפאו"ש והבריאות גופא נהורא מעליא, ולזכות כלל ישראל.

בכבוד ואהבה,
אברהם יעקב הכהן פאם

The letter to Rabbi Sherer

When Rabbi Sherer passed away on the day of Agudath Israel's annual dinner in the spring of 1998, it was decided not to inform Rav Pam until after the funeral, for he was then quite ill and in constant pain, and walking was extremely difficult for him. During the funeral, it became known that Rav Pam was across the street in a building where there was an audio hook-up (for as a *kohen* he could not enter the building where the funeral was taking place). To everyone's surprise, Rav Pam came prepared to deliver his own *hesped*, despite the excruciating pain that he was suffering. A microphone was set up, and from there, Rav Pam's tearful words were amplified to the tens of thousands in the street and in the building where the actual funeral was held.

Rav Pam assumed that his *hesped* would be the last one at the funeral. As he made his way to the exit following his *hesped*, yet another speaker was announced over the loudspeakers. Rav Pam immediately turned around and returned to his seat, to show respect for Rabbi Sherer and for the speaker.

The Tenth Siyum HaShas

One of Rav Pam's most memorable public addresses took place at the tenth *siyum* of the Daf Yomi cycle on 26 Elul, 5757 (September 28, 1997). Knowing that Madison Square Garden alone would not be able to accomodate the tens of thousands of participants, Agudath Israel also leased the Nassau Coliseum. The Siyum program originated out of both sites and was linked via satellite to gatherings across North America and beyond. Rav Pam was asked to deliver the *pesichah* (opening) of the new Daf Yomi cycle from the Coliseum podium.

Rav Pam opened his address by speaking about the great accomplishment of completing all of *Shas*.

> *I wonder whether those who succeeded in learning through Shas fully realize how much they have accomplished! I do not know if a person can truly*

Addressing the Tenth Siyum HaShas of Daf Yomi

comprehend what he has achieved by learning a page of Gemara. And learning a complete masechta! ... How the neshamah radiates with Torah, how a person is elevated! How much spiritual pleasure and joy is brought to one's ancestors, grandparents, great-grandparents in Gan Eden ...

The Vilna Gaon said: Every word of Torah is a mitzvah unto itself. How many words are there on a page of Gemara, in a volume, in the entire Talmud? How great is your accomplishment!

Chinuch Atzmai

In the mid-1970s, Rav Pam joined the *Nesius* (Presidium) of Chinuch Atzmai (Torah Schools for Israel), the primary network of yeshivos and Bais Yaakovs in Eretz Yisrael. It was the Chazon Ish who had declared, "Without Chinuch Atzmai, it would be impossible to live in the Land." Rav Pam was a very active member of the *Nesius* and spoke publicly on the organization's behalf.

When Rav Pam joined the *Nesius*, Chinuch Atzmai's *Nasi* (President) was the leader of the American yeshivah world, Rabbi Moshe Feinstein. In Adar of 5746 (1986), R' Moshe passed away. Shortly thereafter, other *Nesius* members implored Rav Pam to succeed R' Moshe as the organization's *Nasi*. He felt that he could not refuse them.

At a Moetzes Gedolei HaTorah meeting in the home of Rabbi Moshe Feinstein. At table (right to left): Reb Moshe, Rabbi Yaakov Yitzchak Ruderman, Rabbi Moshe Horowitz (Bostoner Rebbe), and Rav Pam.

Rabbi Elazar Menachem Shach

At the annual dinner of Chinuch Atzmai at which Rav Pam was officially installed as *Nasi*, he said:

> *I am a soldier and I have been drafted by the gedolei Torah in America. What could I say? — especially after HaGaon HaRav Shach,* שליט"א*, immediately sent his blessings and words of encouragement.*
>
> *When I remind myself who the previous Nasi was, I feel wholly inadequate ... I am not "replacing" R' Moshe in this position — R' Moshe is irreplaceable. I am merely a soldier. I am not a 'Nasi' but a 'nosei' — a* נוֹשֵׂא בְּעוֹל*, one who shares the burden which Chinuch Atzmai carries, a little, in my simple way.*

J.E.P.

In 1973, Agudath Israel's Jewish Education Program (J.E.P.) was founded, to reach out to Jewish public school children in the New York area and beyond. Rav Pam was consulted regularly whenever questions would arise on how to run the program. "Rav Pam was always such a positive force, always so full of advice and encouragement," says Rabbi Mutty Katz, the program's National Director.

Rav Pam recognized the hidden potential of every Jewish child

One of J.E.P.'s very successful *kiruv* (outreach) tools is its "Release Hour" program where yeshivah students spend an hour a week studying Torah with public school students. When this program was first tested at the beis midrash of Torah Vodaath, some were concerned. "Could this perhaps tarnish the yeshivah's reputation, to have so many long-haired, leather-jacketed boys milling around in our beis medrash?"

Rav Pam was not the least bit concerned. "Only good can come from this," he assured everyone.[3] He would greet the boys personally when they came to the yeshivah.

3. On the other hand, when J.E.P. was asked to send yeshivah students to do *kiruv* work in a shul with an invalid *mechitzah*, Rav Pam would not permit it.

Years later, Rav Pam was asked to speak at a special gathering at Yeshivas Ner Yisrael in Baltimore. When he returned from his trip, he told Rabbi Katz, "I have regards for you from ____." Rabbi Katz did not recognize the name.

Rav Pam smiled. "He said that you would not know his name. He was a 'Release Hour' student who would come to Torah Vodaath once a week. He was so inspired that the following summer when he visited Eretz Yisrael, he entered a yeshivah every now and then and asked people to learn with him. When he graduated high school, he decided to 'take off a year' before entering college, so that he could experience the joy of full-time Torah learning. He enrolled in Ner Yisrael and he's been learning there ever since!"

Be'er HaGolah

In 1979, Rav Pam played a key role in the founding of Be'er HaGolah, the first yeshivah in America for Russian immigrant children. Rav Pam was deeply involved with the school until the end of his life.

Visiting a class at Be'er HaGolah

Until illness made it too difficult, Rav Pam would visit Be'er HaGolah often. He would test the students, encourage them and speak with the school administration and teachers. Usually he was invited to come, but sometimes he came on his own, accompanied by his rebbetzin. Teachers and students saw him as their guide and inspiration.

When "*chavrusa* programs" were arranged between boys from Be'er HaGolah and Torah Vodaath talmidim, Rav Pam would walk around the Torah Vodaath beis midrash greeting the boys and showing an interest in what they were learning.

Rav Pam emphasized the importance of a good sports program at the school and upon his suggestion, chess — a popular pastime among Russians — was introduced as an activity.

On Purim, the students of Be'er HaGolah come to school in the morning, to hear the reading of the Megillah and to enjoy a true Purim atmosphere. For many years, after the festivities

ended, many rebbeim and *moros* would take their students to the home of Rav Pam, to bring *mishloach manos* to "their Rebbi."

Sometimes, on their own initiative, boys would go to visit Rav Pam. As one student put it, "I know that when Rav Pam talks to me, he really means it."

Once, a Be'er HaGolah graduate who had become engaged asked that Rav Pam serve as her *mesader kiddushin* (officiating rav at a *chuppah*). She explained, "I am part of the Be'er HaGolah family and Rav Pam is our Rebbi."

Nechomas Yisroel

In Elul 5755 (1995), a school in Queens with 400 Russian immigrant children closed down. Seeing no alternative, their parents planned to enroll these children in public schools. Rabbi Usher Friedman, then studying in the kollel of the Nitra Yeshivah, was appalled that such a tragedy was

With the Skulener Rebbe

taking place. He therefore went to discuss this crisis with the Skulener Rebbe, Rabbi Yisrael Portugal. The Rebbe told him, "The leader of *kiruv* (Jewish outreach) is Rav Pam. Go to him for advice." A phone call to Rav Pam led to a private meeting at his home. Soon after, Nechomas Yisroel was founded.

Rav Pam's advice was *not* to open a new school to educate these children. Instead, he suggested that an organization be founded through which everyone could sponsor tuition for such children so that they could attend existing yeshivos.

Before Rabbi Friedman left the house after the meeting had ended, Rav Pam withdrew a house key from his pocket, handed it to Rabbi Friedman and (in the presence of Rebbetzin Pam) told him that he was welcome in his house at any time and could use the key to let himself in. Rabbi Friedman appreciated the gesture but never used the key. However, from that day until Rav Pam took ill two years later, he spoke with Rav Pam on the average of twice a day for guidance in his work. Rav Pam was deeply involved with Nechomas Yisroel until his final days.

In the last months of his life, Rav Pam strained himself to attend a Nechomas Yisroel parlor meeting. He told the meeting's host:

> *Shloime, let me tell you what you are doing by hosting the parlor meeting and supporting Nechomas Yisroel. You have the merit of making Hashem happy. You see, R' Shloime, each and every Jewish child is like Hashem's only child. The intense love that we have for our own children, and the feeling of appreciation we have when someone helps our children, does not come close to the love that Hashem has*

Addressing a Nechomas Yisroel parlor meeting a few months before his passing

for every Jewish child. When you save a Yiddishe neshamah (Jewish soul) and bring it back to Hashem before he or she assimilates, you are bringing one of Hashem's children back to Him.

Can you imagine if one of our children would be lost and someone would bring him back to us? How happy and thankful we would be! Now, imagine the joy and thankfulness of Hashem when, by sponsoring the chinuch of these children, you are bringing them back to Him!

At that parlor meeting, Rav Pam quoted Rabbi Levi Yitzchak of Berditchev, who said, "I have such pleasure from learning *Masechta Nedarim* with the [commentary of the] *Ran*, that if I have *Nedarim* with the *Ran*, I don't need [the reward of] *Olam Haba*." Rav Pam then became emotional as he declared, "And I say, if I merit to bring Jewish children to a life of Torah and mitzvos, the pleasure that I derive when seeing them establish Jewish homes is so great that I don't need *Olam Haba*!"

For Every Jewish Child

Rav Pam's name was revered throughout the Torah world. In the last years of his life, he used his influence to ensure that no child was denied a Torah education.

A family arrived in America from Eretz Yisrael and sought to have their children placed in Torah schools. The boys were accepted into a yeshivah, but the girls were not as fortunate. The family's customs differed from the typical American Torah family, the girls spoke only Hebrew and the father made it clear that he could not pay any tuition at all. No school was eager to accept these children.

Time passed and the situation remained unchanged. One day, someone told the father, who was totally unfamiliar with the American yeshivah world, "I suggest that you visit Rabbi Pam; he is a famous tzaddik and will surely help you."

The father wasted no time. He inquired as to where the tzaddik lived and that day, accompanied by his daughters, he rang Rav Pam's doorbell.

This was in Rav Pam's final years, when he was ill and often in pain. Nevertheless, he came to the door and graciously welcomed the family in. After the father explained the problem, Rav Pam took a Chumash and asked one of the girls, age eleven, to read for him. She read beautifully. "I love it!" Rav Pam exclaimed. The father said that in Eretz Yisrael, this girl had belonged to a group that recited the entire Book of Tehillim every Shabbos. Suddenly, the girl burst into tears. "What is wrong?" Rav Pam asked. "I want to go to school," the child replied in Hebrew.

"אַל תִּדְאֲגִי" (Do not worry), Rav Pam responded. "*Today*, you will be in a school." He named a local girls school and told the father to go there immediately with his daughters. By the time they arrived there, Rav Pam had already called. The school administration welcomed them warmly and placed them in appropriate classes. The girls excelled and the school never regretted their decision.

Once, a mesivta menahel came to the conclusion that a certain boy had to be expelled. However, realizing the seriousness of his decision, he phoned Rav Pam to make sure that it was correct. Upon hearing the details, Rav Pam asked to meet the *bachur*. After the meeting, Rav Pam told the menahel, "Keep him in the yeshivah on my *achrayus*," meaning that he accepted responsibility for the boy's behavior. Rav Pam stayed in touch with the boy and because of this, the boy improved and the yeshivah was happy with his performance.

Rav Pam once said, "To me, one of the greatest things that a person can do in his lifetime is to dedicate his life for *Klal Yisrael* — not to live for oneself, but to live for others. This is the [true] measure of a person."

Rav Pam certainly lived by these words.

CHAPTER SIX

In the previous chapter, we saw how Rav Pam devoted so much of his time and energy for the Torah education of Jewish children. Without a doubt, Rav Pam's crowning achievement in this area was his founding and guiding of Shuvu/Return, the organization for the education of Russian immigrant children in Eretz Yisrael. Rav Pam referred to Shuvu as "my passport to *Olam Haba*."

He also said, "When I go to the World of Truth and they ask me what I accomplished, I will tell them that I helped to start Shuvu."

Rav Pam's "battle cry" in promoting Shuvu was: חִנּוּךְ קוֹדֶשׁ לְזֶרַע קוֹדֶשׁ בְּאֶרֶץ הַקוֹדֶשׁ, *An education of holiness for holy children in the Holy Land.*

A Movement Is Born

Shuvu[1] was founded in 1990. In its 16-year existence, this Torah network has experienced growth which is clearly לְמַעְלָה מִדֶּרֶךְ הַטֶּבַע, *beyond the plane of nature.* Shuvu currently provides over 16,000 children with a Torah education each year.

Until his passing, Rav Pam was involved in every important decision relating to the organization. R' Avraham Biderman,

At the meeting of rabbanim at which Shuvu was officially founded: Rav Pam, the Boboover Rebbe (seated next to podium) and יבל"ח *Rabbi Avraham Chaim Spitzer (speaking); the Skulener Rebbe (far left).*

1. The name שׁוּבוּ/Shuvu is based on the verses: וְדוֹר רְבִיעִי יָשׁוּבוּ הֵנָּה, *And the fourth generation shall return here (Bereishis* 15:16); and וְשָׁבוּ בָנִים לִגְבוּלָם, *And the children will return to their border (Yirmiyahu* 31:16).

The Gerrer Rebbe

Rabbi Yosef Sholom Elyashiv

Shuvu's co-Chairman of the Board, who is in daily contact with the organization's administration in Eretz Yisrael, consulted with Rav Pam every day. When the need arose, Rav Pam would contact *gedolim* in Eretz Yisrael, including Rabbi Aharon Leib Steinman; the present Gerrer Rebbe, Rabbi Yaakov Aryeh Alter; and Rabbi Shmuel Auerbach. From Shuvu's founding until today, Rabbi Yosef Sholom Elyashiv's guidance has often been sought.

Rabbi Shmuel Auerbach

Rabbi Aharon Leib Steinman,
Rav Pam, Avraham Biderman

"I Am With You!"

When it was time to build the Second Beis HaMikdash, the Jews encountered difficulties and were discouraged. Hashem told them through Chaggai HaNavi, "וַעֲשׂוּ, כִּי אֲנִי אִתְּכֶם נְאֻם ה׳", "*And do, for I am with you — the word of Hashem*" (*Chaggai* 2:4). At Shuvu gatherings, Rav Pam would often mention these words of Chaggai. He would say that those who head Shuvu should not be afraid to start new schools due to lack of money. If Russian immigrant parents were asking for such a school, they could not be told, "No." The answer would have to be "Yes," and somehow, Hashem would help.

Once, as Pesach approached, Shuvu found itself hundreds of thousands of dollars short of the payroll needed to pay its teachers before Yom Tov. When someone expressed concern

about the situation, Rav Pam responded, "What are you worried about? We are doing what the *Ribono shel Olam* wants; He will surely help us." Soon after, Shuvu received a single donation which covered the deficit for that payroll.

At one point, when the organization experienced a very serious financial crisis, a meeting of some 15 wealthy donors was held in Rav Pam's home. Rav Pam declared, "Until now, we have been going forward. Are we now going to go backwards?" And he began to cry.

That meeting was a huge success.

More than Tzedakah

Rav Pam would say that Shuvu was more than *tzedakah*. It was a "movement" to change the face of Eretz Yisrael, making it a place fit for Hashem to rest His *Shechinah* and build the Third Beis HaMikdash. Rav Pam's understanding of

Rav Pam signing Shuvu checks, which he co-signed together wih Avraham Biderman.

Shuvu's importance to *Klal Yisrael* and Eretz Yisrael prompted him to advise others to earmark significant sums of money for this cause.

A talmid who was not wealthy earned a huge profit in the stock market. When he asked Rav Pam what to do with the shares which he had dedicated for *tzedakah,* he was told, "Give them to Shuvu." The donation totalled $96,000.

One day, he received a phone call from an elderly woman who had recently been widowed. Her husband had left $20,000 for charity. What should she do with it? "Give it to Shuvu," he replied, and she did.

In the spring of 5760 (2000), Rabbi and Mrs. Shmuel Noach Mermelstein suffered the tragic loss of their teenage daughter, Bracha Yitta. The following winter, the first Shuvu girls high school, located in Jerusalem, was dedicated in their daughter's memory. Rav Pam said at that time that it would have been worthwhile to found the organization for this dedication alone.

While Rav Pam made clear that it is a tremendous *zechus* to contribute money to Shuvu, he was careful to point out that other organizations as well are doing great work to bring Jews in Eretz Yisrael closer to Torah. At Shuvu dinners, he would mention the work of Lev L'Achim, Keren Nesivos Moshe and other worthy organizations.

As Fund Raiser

Rav Pam would not hesitate to pick up the phone and call someone to request a donation for Shuvu. One would think that a man so humble would feel uncomfortable requesting a huge donation from a total stranger. But because Rav Pam acted solely *leshem Shamayim* (for the sake of Heaven) and he believed so strongly in this cause and that it was a great *zechus* to have a share in Shuvu's accomplishments, he made such phone calls without hesitation.

People would come to Rav Pam's house to personally deliver sizable donations to Shuvu, to receive his *berachah* and to witness the joy which their donation brought to him. After the person left, Rav Pam would often pick up the phone to call R' Avraham Biderman with the good news.

R' Mordechai Mehlman, Executive Vice-President of Shuvu, would often receive calls from Rav Pam which began, "Mordechai, this is Avraham Pam. I think you will be very happy to come over to my house today. I have a nice 'present' for you." Mr. Mehlman knew exactly what Rav Pam meant — someone had presented him with a generous contribution for Shuvu and he wanted Mr. Mehlman to deposit it.

Not long after Shuvu was founded, Rabbi Chaim Michoel Gutterman, Shuvu's Director in Eretz Yisrael, visited Rav Pam in America and told him of a project for which funds were unavailable. The project called for a weekly evening class in Haifa for girls who were currently attending public school. The hope was that these classes would inspire the girls to attend a religious school the following year. The estimated cost was $800.

Mordechai Mehlman bringing joy to Rav Pam with photos and stories of Shuvu children

With Rabbi Chaim Michoel Gutterman

During his visit, Rabbi Gutterman overheard Rebbetzin Pam's phone conversation in which she was discussing her plans for a trip to Eretz Yisrael. The next day, Rav Pam phoned Rabbi Gutterman to say that he and his rebbetzin had decided that the money which they had planned to use for the rebbetzin's trip should instead be used for the Shuvu project in Haifa. A check made payable to Shuvu had already been written.

Kesher Tefillin

In Shuvu's early years, many of its bar-mitzvah age boys did not own a pair of *tefillin*. Each morning after Shacharis, boys would take turns putting on their friends' tefillin.

Then, R' Binyomin Drew came up with the following idea: When an American yeshivah student becomes a bar mitzvah, his family, in honor of this occasion, should purchase a pair of tefillin for a Shuvu student in Eretz Yisrael. Rav Pam was overjoyed by this suggestion. He said, "Many parents bring their bar mitzvah boys to me. Often, they ask what the boy should do with the *maaser* money which he separates from his bar mitzvah gifts, and I am not sure how to respond. But this [i.e. to purchase tefillin for a Shuvu student] has everything in it!" Immediately, Rav Pam wrote out a personal check to purchase a pair of tefillin. This project became known as *Kesher Tefillin.*[2]

A Shuvu talmid wearing the tefillin sponsored by a yeshivah student in America.

Rav Pam spoke of the enormous *zechus* which a boy acquires when upon becoming a bar mitzvah, he provides another Jewish child with the lifelong opportunity to fulfill the precious mitzvah of tefillin.

Each contributor to the Kesher Tefillin Fund receives a plaque with a photograph of the Shuvu student wearing his new tefillin. When Rav Pam received his plaque, he kissed the photograph and exclaimed, "This boy is wearing tefillin because of me!" The plaque was hung in his living room.

Stories that Touch the Heart

Rav Pam loved to hear stories of the Shuvu children, stories of their *mesiras nefesh* (self-sacrifice) for Torah and mitzvos. As Rabbi Gutterman recalled, "Whenever I would come to visit Rav Pam prior to a Shuvu dinner, he wanted a report on our activities, on the new schools, and he wanted to hear about the children.

2. *Kesher* means "knot," a reference to the *kesher* of the *tefillin shel yad* and *shel rosh;* and it also means "bond," a reference to the bond that this project creates between the Shuvu students and young *bnei Torah* in America.

With a Shuvu student

"It happened not once or twice, not ten times — but more — that Rav Pam and his rebbetzin sat and cried as they listened to the greatness of these children. It gave him such *chizuk* (encouragement)."

Below are two such stories:

A third-grade girl was her teacher's guest for the Shabbos meal on Friday evening. Toward the end of the meal, they heard the honking of a car horn; it was the girl's non-religious parents who had come to take her home. The teacher felt terrible. She thought that her efforts for this child were being wasted.

The teacher wished her student *"Shabbat Shalom,"* and watched sadly from the window as the child walked to the waiting car. And then, to her amazement and delight, she watched as the car drove slowly down the street while the child walked home alongside it.

Today this girl is married to a *ben Torah* who studies in a kollel.

An eleven-year-old-boy was keeping all the mitzvos, while his parents did not. His mother arranged for him to receive private lessons in English, to take place on Shabbos. The boy could not convince his mother to change the appointment. He therefore slammed a door against his hand so that the injury would prevent him from writing on Shabbos.

Rav Pam, with his own pure heart, recognized the hidden greatness in these children when he founded Shuvu. And he cried tears of joy as he saw his dream becoming a reality.

A Petition from Russian Parents

Each summer, a major parlor meeting for Shuvu is held in Brooklyn in the home of Mr. and Mrs. Gedaliah Weinberger. In the days before the 1999 summer parlor meeting, Rav Pam was extremely ill. Unknown to the public, plans were being made for Rav Pam to address the meeting from his home via satellite transmission. But on the day of the meeting he insisted on attending; special preparations were necessary to make this possible. He was confined to bed for a week before the meeting. A few days after the meeting he fell, probably due to weakness. He was in agony and needed two weeks of bed rest to recover. He later said, "I knew that I would pay a price, but I have no regrets."

Prior to that meeting, Rabbi Gutterman sent Rav Pam a report on Shuvu activities and ideas for expansion. To the

A Shuvu parlor meeting in Rav Pam's final years.
Rabbi Matisyahu Salomon is at left.

report he attached a petition from 120 parents in Natzereth-Ilit, requesting a Shuvu school in their city. Rabbi Gutterman added a personal note that Shuvu was at a crossroads, because the potential for expansion was great, but there was a shortage of money. On paper, it appeared that the request from Natzereth-Ilit would have to be denied.

Rav Pam issued a heartfelt plea at that parlor meeting:

> *There is a petition from 120 parents asking for a Shuvu school in Natzeret-Ilit. It's stirring; it's heart-rending. They plead: "We don't want to send our children to the secular schools. We want a Shuvu school for our children. Please open a school."*
>
> *But a report I received says: "The way things seem, we will be forced to say, 'No,' as it seems unfeasible that we will be able to fund new schools."*

> *We will be forced to say, "No," to these parents. "Sorry — your children will have to go to public school."*
>
> *Yes, we are having a hard time raising funds for the current budget. It seems that we are forced to say, "No." But, my dear brothers and friends, there is an overriding, irresistible force to say, "Yes!"*
>
> *And I say right now, "Dear parents — Yes! There will be a school opened in Natzeret-Ilit. And the Shechinah (Divine Presence) will be in that school."*
>
> *No calculation in the world can make us say, "No." The Ribono shel Olam will just have to provide the means somehow.*
>
> *They're begging and we are going to say, "No"?*
>
> *If we turn them down, will we be able to live with ourselves? Will this not haunt us for the rest of our lives?*
>
> *There is only one answer: We must call Reb Chaim Michoel Gutterman and say — "Yes! Open up the school! Take them in!"*
>
> *We want the children in Torah schools so that the Shechinah will be there, protecting the children, hovering over them, blessing them — and their parents as well.*

That parlor meeting was an overwhelming success. One man who was far from wealthy looked at his check register, saw that he had a balance of $515, and wrote out a check for that amount.

In His Honor

No words can describe the atmosphere at Shuvu dinners when Rav Pam spoke. One truly felt that שְׁכִינָה מְדַבֶּרֶת מִתּוֹךְ גְּרוֹנוֹ, the *Shechinah* was speaking from within him.

Rav Pam was Guest of Honor at the 10th anniversary dinner of Shuvu in February 2001. It was to be the last Shuvu dinner of his life. In the months preceding the dinner, his health took

Addressing a Shuvu gathering in the organization's early years

an alarming turn for the worse. He was weak and his feet were swollen due to kidney problems.

The dinner was held on the 19th of Shevat. Four days earlier, he told a talmid, "This morning, I was extremely dizzy. All my life, I never felt like that."

"How will Rebbi go to the dinner?" his talmid asked.

"I *must* go; there is no choice," Rav Pam replied.

He wore a new pair of shoes to the dinner, for his old shoes were too small for his swollen feet. Rebbetzin Pam, always concerned for her husband's welfare, asked him to shorten his speech, to which he replied, "I have a lot to say."

Greeting a guest at a Shuvu dinner

He met with R' Avraham Biderman prior to the dinner. "They are honoring me," he said, "but I know that it is really all the people who work for Shuvu whom they are honoring." He then asked Mr. Biderman to help him compile a list of all those whose names should be mentioned in his address.

As Rav Pam entered the Ateres Chayah ballroom that night, supported by two grandsons, the crowd of more than 1000 rose to its feet as the musician played, *"Yamim al*

With the Novominsker Rebbe

yemei melech tosif..."[3] It was a moment that no one present will ever forget.

A Shuvu talmid, 19-year-old Eliezer Feldman, was flown in from Eretz Yisrael to speak in Rav Pam's honor. At the conclusion of his speech, he presented Rav Pam with a scroll of thanks signed by all the thousands of children enrolled in the Shuvu schools. The scroll was unfurled behind the dais along half the length of the ballroom.

The next speaker was Rabbi Yaakov Perlow, the Novominsker Rebbe, who expressed the feelings of everyone.

> *I think that all will agree that this dinner serves as an opportunity to express to Rav Pam what our entire generation of Torah Jews feels about him. Our generation sees in him that blend, that*

3. "May You add days onto the days of the King [may his years be like all generations]" — *Tehillim* 61:7.

light of Torah, tzidkus, chesed and emes that few people merit.

... The crowning gift of Rav Pam to all of us has been the vision of Shuvu, the movement of וְשָׁבוּ בָנִים לִגְבוּלָם *(And the children will return to their border); ... We thank the Ribono shel Olam that Rav Pam is with us here tonight to celebrate the reality of this dream; and to inspire us to go from strength to strength.*

"How Can I Thank You...?"

Rav Pam was introduced as the next speaker. He began by expressing his feelings at seeing the overflow crowd that had assembled in his honor. Then he said in a tear-choked voice:

> *Ribono shel Olam, how can I thank You for the zechus that You gave me, the daas (wisdom) to intitiate and to launch Shuvu? ... How can I express even a fraction of my gratitude to HaKadosh Baruch Hu for granting me such a zechus and for granting the entire Shuvu family this zechus?*
>
> *[And how can I thank HaKadosh Baruch Hu], for the truly incredible siyata diShmaya at every step. We often quoted the words of Chaggai HaNavi, who said,"*וַעֲשׂוּ, כִּי אֲנִי אִתְּכֶם נְאוּם ה'*", "And do, for I am with you — the word of Hashem ..." This has been our slogan, "Just do, for I [Hashem] am with you!" And we have seen it all along the way ...*

Rabbi Shlomo Feivel Schustal greets Rav Pam at a Shuvu Dinner. Rabbanim and roshei yeshivah made a special effort to attend the Shuvu dinner in Rav Pam's honor. Even after his passing, the dais at Shuvu dinners is still graced by great Torah personalities.

... I accept this honor tonight as a shaliach tzibur (representative) of all those who, without them, Shuvu would not have happened. They are very, very involved with Shuvu and it is to their credit that Shuvu exists ... Everyone, including the supporters, is part of the Shuvu movement and I am only a shaliach tzibur sharing the honor with the entire Shuvu family. It's a family, a teamwork, we all work together and the Ribono shel Olam is with us. וַעֲשׂוּ, כִּי אֲנִי אִתְּכֶם!

... There is so much more to do — and we have to do it, along with the other organizations and individuals who are doing this type of work. Baruch Hashem, we are on the march; Torah is on the march.

Ribono shel Olam, just give us a little more time and we will present You with an Eretz Yisrael that is a palace fit for the King to return to. Give us a little more time, give us siyata diShmaya to accomplish what we are set to accomplish, for Your honor.

Borei kol Olamim (Creator of all Worlds): Give us more time and siyata diShmaya and You will see what kind of Eretz Yisrael You will have, what kind of children You will have. "וְכָל בָּנַיִךְ לִמּוּדֵי ה'", And all your children will be students of Hashem" (Yeshayahu 54:13).

Source of Strength

Rav Pam's deep involvement with Shuvu continued even during the final months of his life when he was dreadfully weak and spent many days in the hospital. At times, he could barely speak or extend his hand. Yet, he drew strength — literally — from hearing good news about Shuvu.

One day, R' Avraham Biderman came to the hospital and brought along a copy of a check made out to Shuvu — a donation of *one million dollars*. This news seemed to give Rav Pam strength; he took hold of the copy and continued to grasp it for a long time.

There was something else from which he drew strength in a seemingly miraculous way — letters from Shuvu children in which they wrote of mitzvos which they had accepted upon themselves as a source of merit for Rav Pam's recovery. When Rabbi Gutterman heard of the effect that these letters had on Rav Pam, he arranged for a daily mailing of letters to America.

Source of the Miracle

At the 2005 Shuvu summer parlor meeting, Rabbi Matisyahu Salomon said:

We are awed by the miracles. The children. The teachers. How schools start ... It's all nissim.

But the greatest miracle is that the children are eager to learn and live Torah — and their parents allow this. I have been to Russia. I have seen the children there. I have seen people brainwashed so that they simply cannot accept religion.

How does this miracle come about? How can it be that these Jews, so distant from Yiddishkeit, suddenly embrace Torah and mitzvos?

With Rabbi Matisyahu Salomon

The answer is that as the Chazon Ish taught, one Jew can daven that another Jew should do teshuvah.

We all remember Rav Pam's begging Hashem to help the children from Russia come close to Him. We saw his pain and anguish as he embraced those neshamos from the distance. I am convinced that the miracle of Shuvu's success is rooted in those tefillos while he was alive, and even more so now that he is in front of Hashem's Throne.

How fitting that after Rav Pam's passing, the organization was officially renamed in his memory *Shuvu — Chazon Avraham* (Shuvu — the Vision of Avraham). As his son R' Dovid pointed out, the Torah is called *"Toras Moshe"* because Moshe Rabbeinu was willing to undertake any sacrifice for the sake of the Torah.

Displaying the proclamation of gedolei Yisrael renaming the organization Shuvu-Chazon Avrohom. Left to right: Moshe Fuchs, Avraham Biderman (partially obscured) Rabbi Aharon Pam, Rabbi Heshy Arem, Mordechai Mehlman.

In a similar sense, Rav Pam was willing to sacrifice anything — even his health — for the sake of Shuvu.

"Shuvu's impact in Eretz Yisrael is enormous," says Rabbi Chaim Michoel Gutterman. "What we are seeing now is *'Chazon Avraham.'* This is what Rav Pam foresaw when others thought that it could not be done."

CHAPTER SEVEN

A Wellspring of Chesed

It was only a few minutes after *havdalah* when the phone rang in Rav Pam's home. The caller was a sad, lonely individual and Rav Pam was obviously distressed as he listened to the caller pour out his troubles. "No, no, no!" he told the caller. "How can you say that you have no friends? I'm your friend!"

Despite Rav Pam's very busy schedule as a rebbi, Rosh HaYeshivah and leader of *Klal Yisrael,* he found time to help countless individuals, many of whom were total strangers when they first came to see him.

Once, someone came to speak to him in yeshivah after Minchah. Rav Pam was obviously busy, so the person said, "Perhaps the Rosh Yeshivah does not have time now?" Rav Pam replied, "One never has time, but one must make time when it comes to helping someone else. If you don't make time, *you'll never have time*, because people are always busy."

A House of Chesed

Rav Pam's home was one of *chesed*, both great and small.

A former talmid who was in Rav Pam's eleventh-grade class some *50 years ago* remained in touch with him throughout the decades that followed. Once, he and his wife made an appointment to visit Rav and Rebbetzin Pam. When they drove up in front of the Pam home, they found Rebbetzin Pam waiting outside for them. Parking spaces in the neighborhood are difficult to find, so Rebbetzin Pam had secured permission for the couple to park in a neighbor's driveway — and she had waited outside to inform them of this.

When the visit drew to a close, Rav Pam and his rebbetzin walked their guests out the door. "It's not necessary for the Rosh Yeshivah to do this," the talmid protested. Rav Pam responded with a smile, "It's part of *hachnasas orchim* (welcoming guests) and my name is Avraham!" "And mine is Sarah!" the Rebbetzin added.[1]

For the Lonely and the Sad

Rav Pam taught his talmidim:

A person can do *chesed* with a smile or a friendly word. There are simple people to whom others pay no attention. Most people just walk past them without ever saying, "Good morning," or "How are you?" When someone pays attention to such people and relates to them in a friendly way, they feel honored and have tremendous pleasure from this.

And there are people, said Rav Pam, who are sad and even depressed. When someone speaks to their hearts and eases their pain, he has performed a great *chesed*.

Every afternoon when he was not delivering his *shiur*, Rav Pam was at his seat in the Torah Vodaath beis midrash. His official purpose for being there was to be available for talmidim who wanted to discuss either their learning or personal matters. But as the years passed, more and more of Rav Pam's time was taken up by outsiders. People from all walks of life would come to discuss personal and communal matters with him.

One day, the Menahel, Rabbi Yitzchak Yaakov Sekula, approached Rav Pam and said: "The talmidim need the Rosh Yeshivah. A few of them have gotten together and volunteered to ask outsiders who enter the beis midrash to refrain from disturbing the Rosh Yeshivah during *seder* (learning sessions)." Rav Pam replied that he would have to think the matter through.

1. Avraham Avinu and Sarah Imeinu excelled in *chesed*.

Rabbi Yitzchak Yaakov Sekula, Rabbi Lipa Margulies, Rav Pam, Yonah Blumenfrucht

A few days later, he told Rav Sekula, "I have thought it over. No, I cannot agree to the suggestion. These people have no one to listen to them. There are so many problems, Rav Sekula, and they need someone to hear them out! There is no choice; I must be available for them."

Said Rav Sekula, "It pained him that he had to take time away from being available for talmidim and from his learning. This was his life! For him, this was true *mesiras nefesh* (self-sacrifice), for his *nefesh* (soul) was bound to the Torah and to his talmidim."

His "Friends"

During their years in East New York, the Pams were acquainted with Benny L., a high-functioning mentally disabled man who lived alone. At that time, Benny spoke with

Rav Pam, either by phone or in person, almost every day. In 1984, the Pams were instrumental in having Benny accepted into a Women's League Community Residence for Jewish men like himself. From that time, Benny, whose days were now very productive, "had time to speak with Rav Pam only occasionally." Upon hearing the news of Rav Pam's passing, Benny called the Women's League main office and told them, "I lost my best friend, Rabbi Pam. Now, I have a pain in my heart."

Some 25 years ago, a certain elderly woman lived alone in an apartment building near Mesivta Torah Vodaath. She was a frequent guest at the Shabbos table of Rav and Rebbetzin Pam. This woman once told a Torah Vodaath talmid that she had two "friends" in Torah Vodaath — Rav Pam and Rav Gedaliah Schorr.

Years ago, there was a homeless fellow who would often take refuge in the Torah Vodaath beis midrash. The man wore old, dirty clothing and most people found it difficult to be near him. Rav Pam not only befriended the man, but would sometimes take him to his home to provide him with a meal.

One Tishah B'Av evening after *Eichah* had been read and everyone was filing out of the beis midrash in the Torah Vodaath *minyan*, a talmid approached Rav Pam to discuss something. Rav Pam, however, seemed preoccupied, so the talmid turned to leave — but then something caught his eye. Rav Pam took a box of matzah and some hard-boiled eggs and placed them out of view in the women's section. Then he went over to the homeless man, and whispered into his ear. The man went behind the curtain to take his food. Apparently, Rav Pam was concerned that the man would have nothing on which to break his fast the following night.

Mitzvah Celebrations

As a Rosh Yeshivah, rebbi and leader of *Klal Yisrael*, Rav Pam was invited to many, many *simchas*. Once, someone remarked to him in jest, "A yeshivah really needs three roshei yeshivah; one to deliver *shiurim*, one to raise funds and one to attend *simchas*." Rav Pam smiled and replied, "And I am the one who attends *simchas*!"

When he received an invitation, he tried his best to attend, especially if it was a talmid's *simchah*.

During the year of mourning following his mother's passing, Rav Pam would go to weddings for a few minutes to wish the *chasan* "Mazel tov" and offer his *berachah*, prior to the chuppah ceremony. Some weeks this was a nightly occurrence, and some nights he went to more than one wedding. Someone asked him, "It is such an effort for the Rosh Yeshivah to go to these weddings, and people know that the Rosh Yeshivah is an

Dancing with Rabbi Nosson Wachtfogel at the wedding of a talmid

avel (mourner) and can only stay for a short while — must he take the time every night just to say 'Mazel tov'?"

Rav Pam replied, "For me it's every night, but for the *chasan*, it's once in his lifetime."

Another person's joyous occasion was truly his own. Once, a baby was born to someone who consulted with Rav Pam often. The person decided not to phone Rav Pam with the news. This was in the last years of Rav Pam's life when he was suffering from a number of serious conditions. Around that time, he had taken a turn for the worse, and therefore the person thought it best not to bother Rav Pam.

The next time that the person saw Rav Pam, he mentioned the good news. "Why didn't you come to tell me?" Rav Pam asked. The man replied honestly that he had thought it best not to bother the Rosh Yeshivah.

Rav Pam responded, "You don't understand; the *simchah* that I would have had upon hearing the good news would have given me *chizuk*."

For the Needy

No one will ever know how many poor families were helped by Rav Pam. After his passing, his children were approached by individuals who had received large annual sums from him and were now at a loss without him.

In his last years, he wrote numerous letters requesting *tzedakah* for individuals. When asked why he undertook so many of these mitzvos, he replied by quoting a tzaddik from the previous generation: "For what does the *Ribono shel Olam* need another old Jew, if not that he should do *chesed* with his fellow Jews?"

When Rav Pam turned 83, he remarked to his family that he felt as if he had become a "bar mitzvah," for every day past the age of 70 is a special gift from Hashem.[2] *He felt an enormous responsibility to utilize these years for chesed, as much as his time and energy would allow.*

Once, a man who was raising funds for *hachnasas kallah* asked Rav Pam if he could suggest people whom he could approach for donations. Rav Pam sent him to a local *chesed* organization where he received a sizable donation. A few days later, Rav Pam asked the man what had happened since they last met. "Yes, thank you," he replied. "They gave me a generous check; unfortunately, though, I am still short of my goal."

"In that case," said Rav Pam, "I will give you some of my own money. Please come see me in my home." "No, no," the man protested, "I never intended to ask the Rosh Yeshivah for his own money." Rav Pam, however, saw no reason why he could not participate personally in this mitzvah, and he asked that the man come to his home to receive a donation.

The man, however, did not go. Some time later, the two met on the street. "Why have you not come to me?" asked Rav Pam. "I've been waiting to meet you!" He withdrew a $100 bill from his pocket. "Here," he said, handing it to the man, "I put this aside for you."

Source of Comfort

Rav Pam would often quote the words of Shlomo HaMelech: לְשׁוֹן חֲכָמִים מַרְפֵּא, *The words of wise men*

2. See *Tehillim* 90:10.

heal (*Mishlei* 12:18). He said that to offer kind, healing words is the greatest *chesed* of all.

Especially in the last years of his life, Rav Pam's address was the place to which the sufferings of *Klal Yisrael* were brought. His grandson recalled, "On more than one occasion, I had to leave the room because I could not bear to hear of so much pain, tragedy and anguish in a single day. Yet my grandfather, with his great heart and deep concern for everyone, found the strength to hear such news day in, day out, year after year."

Not that it was easy for him. There were times when Rav Pam needed to lie down because the sad news which he had heard that day simply drained him of his strength.

> *In the summer of 1986, he was not feeling well and was seen by a doctor, who found him to be in good health. "Most probably," said Rav Pam, "I'm weak from the aggravation I suffer when people tell me their tzaros (sufferings)."*
>
> *As Dovid HaMelech said, "Had I not been preoccupied with Your Torah, I would have perished in my suffering" (Tehillim 119:92). When Rav Pam opened a sefer and immersed himself in the waters of Torah, he was in another world, and this infused him with new strength and energy.*

Rav Pam felt the pain of every Jew, even those whom he did not know personally. In his last years, when he learned that a family had suffered the loss of three children in an automobile accident, he insisted on going to comfort the mourners. He had been discharged from the hospital two days earlier. Ignoring his own fragile state of health and his difficulty walking, he traveled by car and then trekked up a steep flight of steps, grasping onto someone for support, to fulfill the mitzvah of *nichum aveilim*.

After he spent some 20 minutes offering words of comfort, the mother said, "Thank you so much, Rosh Yeshivah, for making the effort to come. We know that the Rosh Yeshivah has not been feeling well." Tearfully, Rav Pam replied, "How could I sit back and not come here to share your pain?"

Once, his phone rang late at night, at a time when many had already retired for the night. Rav Pam came to the phone and did his best to help the person with his problem. When he hung up, one of his children asked, "How can a person call so late at night?" "*Nu*," Rav Pam replied, "if only he will sleep peacefully now."

Strengthening the Strong

In October 1994, Nachshon Wachsman, a member of the Israeli Defense Forces, was kidnapped by terrorists.

Five days later, his wicked captors took his life. Throughout the ordeal, Nachshon's parents were interviewed by the Israeli media; always, they spoke with powerful *emunah*, as they stressed that only Hashem could save their son, and they beseeched Jews everywhere to pray for him.

They sanctified Hashem's Name even more by their reaction following their son's murder. R' Yehudah Wachsman uttered his now-famous words:

> *If people will ask why our tefillos were not answered by Hashem in the way that we had hoped, I will tell them: "We did receive a response, we did get an answer. The answer was, 'No,' because sometimes a father can answer, 'No.'"*

Mrs. Esther Wachsman had this to say:

> *The only thing that kept us sane and functioning through all this was our faith. When a person fulfills his mission, then that is the end ... Our faith tells us that these were the years allotted to our son and he fulfilled what he was supposed to fulfill. Our faith is what kept us going.*

In a shmuess delivered at Torah Vodaath soon after this tragic episode, Rav Pam called attention to the world-wide *kiddush Hashem* which the Wachsmans had brought about. Later, someone brought Mrs. Wachsman to Rav Pam when she visited America on behalf of the Shalva organization. Rav Pam spent one half-hour praising her for the *emunah* and *bitachon* which she and her family had demonstrated. In his eyes, he told her, she is a true heroine of our time.

In a letter that he penned in support of the "Beit Nachshon" center which Shalva founded, Rav Pam wrote:

I wish to take this occasion to express my high regard for the parents, Yehuda and Esther Wachsman, because they were מקדש שם שמים ברבים, when in the depth of their צער and aveilus they made a public pronouncement that "Hakodosh Boruch Hu" does indeed hear and heed the תפלות בני ישראל, but a father is also allowed to say sometimes "No!". This was a great, great Kiddush Hashem.
הורים יקרים ונכבדים, בתפילה [illegible] על ידי בנין המקדש [illegible]
ואתם ציון וירושלים ינחם אתכם בכפלים, ובהורים תחיו עד עד!
אברהם יעקב הכהן פאם

Words of chizuk to the parents of Nachshon Wachsman, הי"ד.

I wish to take this occasion to express my high regard for the parents, Yehudah and Esther Wachsman, because they were מְקַדֵּשׁ שֵׁם שָׁמַיִם בְּרַבִּים *when in the depth of their pain they made a public pronouncement that HaKadosh Baruch Hu does indeed hear the tefillos of Bnei Yisrael, but a father is also allowed to sometimes say, "No!" This was a great, great kiddush Hashem.*

A Five-Year Chesed

Ben[3] was born in New York in the 1920s to Orthodox Jewish parents and attended yeshivah. But in his teenage years, he left yeshivah and took to the streets, leaving his religion behind. Eventually, he and a non-Jewish friend opened a store and he settled into a routine, peaceful life.

3. Not his real name.

Some 25 years after Ben left yeshivah, his mother died. Shortly thereafter, she appeared to him in a dream. "Come," she said, "I need you here." He was shaken by the dream and grew even more frightened when the dream recurred a few times.

Ben made a decision. He went to the cemetery, stood before his mother's grave and said, "Ma, you always said that your dream was that I should become a rabbi. I promise you that I *will* become a rabbi."

His first step was to inform his business partner that no longer would he be in the store from Friday afternoon until Saturday night. The partner was furious and threatened to sue. After lawyers were consulted, the issue was resolved with Ben not working on Shabbos and all profits from that day going to his partner.

When he was fully Orthodox once again, Ben moved on to the next part of his plan — to become a talmid chacham and receive *semichah* (rabbinical ordination), to fulfill his promise to his mother.

He made some inquiries and it was suggested that he speak to Rav Pam, who at that time was not yet Rosh HaYeshivah and spent his days teaching and guiding his talmidim. Ben introduced himself to Rav Pam, told him his story and asked if he could teach him privately. Rav Pam said, "I really do not have time, but I cannot say, 'No.' "

With his yeshivah background, Ben progressed quickly. After they had studied together for five years, Rav Pam declared Ben fit to be tested for *semichah.* He arranged for Ben to be tested orally by a certain rav.[4] The rav was satisfied with Ben's knowledge of halachah and granted him *semichah*. Ben returned to the cemetery with his certificate of *semichah* in his hand, stood before his mother's grave and said, "Ma, I've kept my promise."

A Baal Chesed's Pain

In the summer of 1979, Rav Pam delivered a *hesped* for Rav Gedaliah Schorr, who had recently passed away. When the new school semester began, he borrowed a tape of the *hesped* from one of his talmidim. On the morning of Erev Rosh Hashanah, he met the talmid and said that he wished to speak with him after Shacharis. When they met later, Rav Pam was obviously upset. "I would have given anything that it shouldn't happen. I don't know how to make it up to you." The talmid could not imagine to what his rebbi was referring, until he explained that the tape had gotten tangled in the recorder and had torn. The tape was an original, Rav Pam knew, and would be difficult to replace. The talmid assured Rav Pam that he was experienced at unraveling and repairing cassette tapes. Sure enough, after an hour's work, the tape was repaired.

4. Rav Pam explained to Ben why he did not want to be the one to confer the semichah.

That night after Maariv, after wishing Rav Pam, *"Leshanah tovah..."* the talmid said, "I took care of the tape and it's fine." Rav Pam replied, "You can't imagine how happy you have made me. *HaKadosh Baruch Hu* should help that the coming year should be as happy for you as you have made me on this evening."

On Tzom Gedaliah, Rav Pam presented the talmid with a gift — cassette recordings of two of his shmuessen — to show his *hakaras hatov*, and to make up "for all the aggravation" that he had caused him.

A Baal Chesed's Tears

Around a year before Rav Pam passed away, the head of an out-of-town kollel came to consult with him at his home. During their conversation, the young man asked if Rav Pam could suggest well-to-do donors in the New York area whom he could contact, in Rav Pam's name, to pledge support for the kollel.

Rav Pam opened a notebook with names of those whom he would call from time to time to request contributions for Torah

Vodaath, Shuvu and various other causes. He went through the names, one by one, but had a difficult time suggesting anyone to contact. He explained that every person on the list either had recently been asked for *tzedakah*, or was soon to be asked. He could suggest only one individual whom the *rosh kollel* could contact in his name at that time.

In the past when this rosh kollel had visited, Rav Pam would always extend a warm blessing to him when he rose to leave. This time, however, Rav Pam was visibly upset and offered a quiet blessing for success.

The rosh kollel was already out the front door when he suddenly remembered that there was one question that he had forgotten to ask. He rang the doorbell, was admitted by Rebbetzin Pam and made his way up the staircase to Rav Pam's study. He found Rav Pam wiping away his tears. The fact that he had been unable to help the rosh kollel in his quest for donors had brought him to tears.

Small Acts, Big Accomplishments

Rav Pam, quoting the Alter of Novarodok, said that there is a moment in every person's life when he achieves something great, and that moment obligates him to achieve great things for the rest of his life. Rav Pam then related what, to his mind, was such a moment in his own life:

An elderly member of the Mesivta Torah Vodaath minyan took ill and was hospitalized. As a *kohen*, Rav Pam could not visit the man, but he took the time to write him a letter. The man passed away shortly thereafter. Rav Pam was later informed that the man kept the letter under his pillow and whenever a visitor would enter his room, he would take out the letter and show it to him.

Said Rav Pam: "With a simple letter which took but a couple of minutes to write, I lifted the spirits of this man in a way that I had never imagined. This is a lesson to me: what seems to be a small act that takes little time can accomplish great things."

A smile for a lonely soul. A few kind words to a sad, depressed person. A short letter of good wishes to a sick man. These are some of the "small" great things that Rav Pam accomplished — and from which all of us can learn.

CHAPTER EIGHT

A Way with Words

Rav Pam would often quote the Rambam, who teaches us the proper behavior of a talmid chacham:

A talmid chacham does not scream or shout ... He does not raise his voice more than necessary; rather, he speaks pleasantly to all people ... He extends greetings to all so that they are pleased with him ... He judges others favorably ... He speak their praises and never speaks shamefully of others ... He never goes back on his word. In

general, he speaks only words of wisdom and lovingkindness ...

(*Rambam, Hilchos De'os* 5:7).

Rav Pam continued: "*He speaks pleasantly to all people ...* pleasantly, warmly ... *He extends greetings to all ...* even to gentiles, gentile neighbors, gentile maintenance workers in the yeshivah. *He speaks only words of wisdom and lovingkindness* — because words are not *hefker*."

A person would not declare a valuable watch or stereo system "*hefker*" and leave it out in the street for anyone to take. He knows that these items are expensive, and therefore he guards them carefully. Similarly, a Jew has to know that words are not "cheap." The power of speech is a gift from Hashem and we must use this gift wisely, choosing our words carefully and making sure that our words are constructive and not destructive.

The words and sentences, the ideas and advice which Rav Pam uttered, were carefully measured. They flowed from a pure heart and Torah mind working together in perfect harmony.

Musical Notes

Rav Pam's earliest talmidim were convinced that he was American-born because his command of English was outstanding. Furthermore, he had worked hard — and with great success — to eliminate his European accent.

A classmate worked with him night after night to help him perfect *one* pronunciation. Rav Pam later said that he invested

Delivering an address at a Torah Umesorah convention

Notes which Rav Pam wrote for a speech he delivered at an Agudath Israel convention. A writer later used these notes to prepare an English translation of Rav Pam's words.

so much effort in this because he felt that it is a *kiddush Hashem* when a *ben Torah* expresses himself well.

In his later years when he became recognized as one of the *gedolei hador*, Rav Pam was often called upon to address large public gatherings where many in the crowd did not understand Yiddish. At Torah Umesorah conventions, Shuvu dinners and other important events, Rav Pam held his audience spellbound with his passionate, flawless English presentations.

Rav Pam's care with words included the written word. When his Yiddish speech would be transcribed in English for publication in *The Jewish Observer*, the writer would have to present his work to Rav Pam and then together they would review it slowly and carefully. In addition to making corrections when the wording was not exactly what he had had in mind, Rav Pam would also offer grammatical corrections.

Over a 25-year period, Rabbi Matis Blum spent hundreds of hours with Rav Pam preparing his shmuessen and public addresses for publication both in Hebrew and in English. He recalled:

> *On one occasion, after spending 20 to 30 minutes on a single phrase, Rav Pam turned to me and said almost apologetically, "I'm not very musical, but to someone who is musically inclined, even one wrong note can spoil an entire piece. To me, words are like musical notes, and if I don't have the precise word, it can affect the entire message."*

The Chofetz Chaim's Works

Rav Pam coined an expression which he would tell his *talmidim*: כָּל הַפּוֹרֵשׁ מִסִּפְרֵי חָפֵץ חַיִּים כְּפוֹרֵשׁ מִן הַחַיִּים, *Whoever separates himself from the Chofetz Chaim's works is like separating himself from life itself.* He would say that these *sefarim* are unique in that the student feels that the Chofetz Chaim is speaking directly to him, and his doses of *mussar* are easy to digest and are not depressing.

The Chofetz Chaim

When Rav Pam was a young man, he was approached by Rabbi Mendel Zaks, distinguished son-in-law of the Chofetz Chaim, to learn with one of his sons, who was a student at Torah Vodaath. Rav Pam agreed and the two studied together twice a week. Each time that Rabbi Zaks wanted to pay him, Rav Pam politely refused. One day, Rabbi Zaks said, "R' Avraham, you are doing me the greatest favor by learning with my son! Please allow me to show some *hakaras hatov* (gratitude) by paying you."

Rav Pam replied, "Since I was a boy, your father-in-law has learned with me every day — free of charge! Now, I have the opportunity to show him some *hakaras hatov* by learning with his grandson." Rav Pam meant that the Chofetz Chaim's *sefarim*, particularly *Mishnah Berurah*, *Chofetz Chaim* and *Ahavas Chesed*, were his constant companions and had a tremendous impact on his life. Rabbi Zaks accepted this argument and payment was no longer discussed.

In his *tzava'ah* (will), Rav Pam wrote:

> *If my beloved children and precious talmidim want to do something for my good that will bring me*

Rabbi Mendel Zaks, surrounded by talmidim

pleasure in the World to Come, they should study and teach Sefer Chofetz Chaim and Sefer Ahavas Chesed, privately and in public study groups. All his [the Chofetz Chaim's] words are divrei Elokim Chaim (the word of the Living G-d) and one who forsakes them is like one who forsakes life itself. As for one who will study these works often — it will be pleasant [meaning, a great zechus] for him and for me.

אם ירצו בני אהובי ותלמידי חביבי לעשות לי טובה ונח"ר בעוה"ב
ילמדו וילמדו ספרי ח"ח ואהבת חסד, בין ביחיד ובין בחבורה ברבים
כי כל דבריו דברי א"ח והפורש ממנו כפורש מן החיים; והמרבה בזה
ינעם לו ולי.

Excerpt from Rav Pam's tzava'ah

Avoiding Lashon Hara

As a mesivta rebbi, Rav Pam introduced the study of *Sefer Chofetz Chaim* on the laws of *lashon hara*. He did this a half-century ago when few studied *Sefer Chofetz Chaim* and even fewer used it as a text in the classroom.

This is how it began.

In 1952, a number of Rav Pam's ninth-grade talmidim lived in New Jersey and in parts of New York quite a distance from Willamsburg where Torah Vodaath was located. These boys resided in the yeshivah's dormitory from Sunday to Friday and traveled home for Shabbos. Class on Friday ended at 12:30, and some of these boys would leave at about 11:45 to catch the "Fulton Tubes" train (today called the "Path" train).

Rav Pam felt that this was unnecessary, for the train ride was not very long and there was more than enough time after class ended to travel home and prepare for Shabbos. However, he did not want to insist that the *bachurim* leave later.

An additional problem was that these boys would straggle in late on Sunday morning, which also could have been avoided.

One Thursday, a couple of weeks into the school year, Rav Pam announced that he wanted to end each week with something special. Therefore, during the last half-hour of class on Fridays, he would be teaching the classic *mussar* work *Mesilas Yesharim*.

The next day, Friday, the "out-of-towners" left early as usual, but when they returned on Sunday, their classmates raved about the wonderful *shiur* which they had missed. Before long, everyone remained on Friday until the end of class.

A few weeks later, Rav Pam announced that he had decided to begin each week with a half-hour *shiur* in *Sefer Chofetz Chaim*. Within a couple of weeks, everyone was coming on time for class on Sundays.

Rav Pam would teach a few *halachos* to his class and discuss them in very practical terms. For example, he would dwell on how one should react when *lashon hara* is spoken at his parents' Shabbos table. More important, the talmidim learned from his personal example to avoid arguments, hurtful or embarrassing words, and anything else that might offend others.

"Dangerous" Times

There is a "dangerous" hour on Rosh Hashanah, Rav Pam told his talmidim, when a Jew needs to be extra careful.

This is the hour after davening is over, when people are either on their way home, or eating the *seudas yom tov*. At such times, it is common to review the day's happenings. "The *baal tefillah* was too low; you could hardly hear him." "He stretched out the davening too much." "The *baal tokei'ah* didn't blow [the shofar] well this year." "Did you see who bought *Maftir* and how much it cost him?" The above statements are either outright lashon hara, hint to it, or will lead to it. Anyone who wants to preserve the *zechuyos* he earned through his davening and *teshuvah* should avoid such talk, especially on Rosh Hashanah, the Day of Judgment.

After Rav Pam's passing, his family found a personal note written many years before, in which he expressed his deep pain for having mistakenly listened to lashon hara on that day. (The Torah forbids listening to lashon hara — see *Shemos* 23:1 with *Rashi*.) That note makes apparent how seriously Rav Pam viewed this sin, and how rare it was for him to transgress it, even by mistake. Rav Pam ends off the note by saying that he will turn this sad day into a day of happiness by taking certain measures to make sure that he will never again repeat this mistake.

Words that Hurt

One of Rav Pam's most memorable public speeches was on the topic of *ona'as devarim*, uttering words that hurt people's feeling. This is forbidden by the Torah.[1]

Rav Pam said:

> *Over the past few years, so much has been written and said concerning the sin of speaking lashon hara. Many are studying the laws of shemiras halashon (guarding one's tongue) on a daily basis.*

1. *Vayikra* 25:17.

Strengthening ourselves against speaking lashon hara is a key factor in hastening Mashiach's arrival.

However, there is another sin relating to speech about which very little is spoken, and that is ona'as devarim. Lashon hara is evil talk spoken about someone. Ona'as devarim refers to remarks that are hurtful to the person to whom they are spoken. Ona'as devarim can cause a great deal of emotional pain and many tragedies can result fom it. As Shlomo HaMelech said: יֵשׁ בּוֹטֶה כְּמַדְקְרוֹת חָרֶב, *There is one who speaks [harshly] like piercings of a sword (Mishlei 12:18).*

Sometimes, words that cut like swords are spoken deliberately, in anger, with the intent to hurt and cause pain. Perhaps more often, such words are spoken carelessly, without any thought about the damage they will cause. People can say things that are absolutely brutal — insulting remarks and name-calling. This is not uncommon, especially within families. This leaves a tragic imprint upon the neshamah of the one who is being insulted.

On the other hand (as the above pasuk continues), לְשׁוֹן חֲכָמִים מַרְפֵּא, *The tongue of wise men heals.*

Words that Heal

Rav Pam utilized every opportunity to say words that made others feel good. His words had an enormous healing power.

A former talmid brought his teenage son to Rav Pam. The boy was extremely shy and Rav Pam was trying to encourage him to overcome this. He said, "Who would have believed that Avraham Pam would one day get up and speak in front of thousands of people? When I was your age, I could not open my mouth in front of one person!"

One day, Rav Pam was accompanied on his walk home from Torah Vodaath by a young man who was carrying a cellular phone. As they walked, the man received a call from his brother living in Israel. From the conversation, it was obvious that the brother was not living a Torah life. When the call ended, Rav Pam said in his typical soft-spoken manner, "It can happen in the best of families." Rav Pam understood that the man may have been embarrassed to have received this call in his presence, so he did his best to put the man at ease.

He made people feel good in other ways. Once, he was walking in a funeral procession when someone introduced him to a man who had helped thousands of poor people. Rav Pam felt that a funeral was not an appropriate place to greet this man and congratulate him on his wonderful work. Instead, he put his arm around the man and, in this way, the two walked down the street.

The Right Word

On the morning of Shavuos, Rebbetzin Pam prepared *kiddush* and mentioned that the honey cake had been prepared by her daughter-in-law. Rav Pam sampled a piece and said, "Please tell her that I had a piece for *kiddush*, that it was delicious and that I thank her very much."

A rosh yeshivah had worked on an important project to benefit *Klal Yisrael*. He was asked to present the project

In 1984, members of the Moetzes Gedolei HaTorah met with Governor Mario Cuomo of New York to express their dismay over the decline of moral values in America. Seated alongside Rav Pam are (left to right): Rabbi Elya Svei, Rabbi Yaakov Perlow (Novominsker Rebbe) and Rabbi Aharon Schechter. Rabbi Moshe Sherer is seated alongside Governor Cuomo.

before the *Moetzes Gedolei HaTorah* (Council of Torah Sages) for approval. The *gedolim* unanimously endorsed the rosh yeshivah's work and as he left the meeting room, Rav Pam said to him, *"Gebencht zolt ir zein"* (May you be blessed)." Years later, the rosh yeshivah still recalled those words of *chizuk*.

At the conclusion of parlor meetings, Rav Pam would ask to speak to the hostess, to thank her for her efforts. Once, he complimented the hostess on some paintings which he had noticed in a side room. The woman said that it was the first time anyone had ever commented about those paintings.

Rav Pam was extremely careful in the way he offered criticism.

A grandson who had recently become a bar-mitzvah walked into the Torah Vodaath beis midrash with his hat tilted sharply forward, imitating the "cool" look. Rav Pam motioned for him to come over and said warmly, "You have such a beautiful forehead; it's a shame to cover it."

Compliments

Rav Pam made a point of complimenting others for a job well done, for he knew that this would encourage them to do well in the future.

After hearing a talmid speak at the *pidyon haben* of his son, Rav Pam told him, "I enjoyed your *dvar Torah* and I can see that you are *shteiging* (progressing) in your learning." These words meant far more than a simple *"Yasher koach."*

A former talmid visited Rav Pam and engaged him in an hour-long Gemara discussion. When the talmid rose to leave, Rav Pam said, "Thank you — it was so *geshmak* (pleasurable)! I enjoyed it!"

The first time that a certain talmid chaired a Torah Vodaath dinner, Rav Pam approached him at the close of the program and said warmly, "I didn't know you had it in you!" As his talmid recalls, "That comment was so perfectly placed and meant so much to me."

At a pidyon haben

A former talmid who was soon to begin his teaching career confided to Rav Pam that he was worried that he would not do well. The night before the beginning of the school year, Rav Pam called him to say, "Don't worry. You will do well." The talmid was moved by his rebbi's thoughtfulness and *chizuk*.

Speaking to his talmidim on Purim

To a talmid who today is a great teacher of Torah, Rav Pam once said, "May you derive as much pleasure from your talmidim as I derive from mine."

He also gave encouragement through action. When a talmid came to his home to say "Goodbye" before leaving for Eretz Yisrael to study Torah, Rav Pam escorted him two blocks to his car. When the talmid suggested that he was now obligated to escort his rebbi back home, Rav Pam replied, "No, you are the one who is going on a journey and it is I who must escort you." The feeling of that escort remained with the talmid throughout the next two years when he was away from his rebbi.

A *bachur* studying in the Torah Vodaath beis midrash led the choir at the Torah Vodaath annual melaveh malkah. At the performance's conclusion, Rav Pam rose from his seat and kissed his talmid on the forehead.

Refined Speech

Rav Pam would say that in his mother's 93 years, an improper word or expression never escaped her lips. "She did not hear shmuessen on the subject," he said. "When she spoke, it was an expression of her pure *neshamah*."

Rav Pam wrote:

> *A refined soul speaks in a refined way. Lashon nekiah (refined speech) is a sign of a pure mind and a refined neshamah. As the Vilna Gaon wrote: "The mouth is kodesh kodashim (holiest of holies)." He also writes that Heavenly angels accompany a person wherever he goes and record his every word.*

Therefore, a Jew should be very careful with his speech at all times, as when speaking before a king.

Darkness and Light

In a shmuess on refined speech, Rav Pam felt forced to utter expressions that should never be uttered by a *ben Torah*.

> *Certain expressions tear at one's ears. For example, "Shut up" — it's difficult for me to say these expressions but I must do so l'toeles (for a constructive purpose).*
>
> *"You did a lousy job" — is that how a ben Torah, or any Jew for that matter, speaks?*
>
> *Certainly, calling someone a "fool," a "moron," an "animal," is far from lashon neki'ah.*

Delivering a shmuess in the main beis midrash of Mesivta Torah Vodaath

When the Chazon Ish heard someone say, "That's a lie!" he said, "Better to say, 'That is not true.'" We may add that far worse than saying, "That's a lie!" is to say, "You're a liar!"

Once, a talmid and his young son accompanied Rav Pam on a Shabbos afternoon walk. When the child ripped a leaf off a branch, his father said, "You're not allowed to do that on Shabbos." Rav Pam turned to his distinguished talmid and said, "It's better to tell him, 'Tomorrow you will be able to do that.'"

In one shmuess, Rav Pam added a new word to the list of those that should not pass our lips: "whatchamicallit." He said, "*Veleche sort vort is dos?*" ("What kind of word is this?")

Later, a talmid asked, "What's wrong with 'whatchamicallit'?"

Rav Pam replied, "Don't you understand? How can you speak without thinking? If you don't know what you want to say, then think. But what kind of a word is 'watchamicallit'?"

The Words of the Wise

Shlomo HaMelech taught: דִּבְרֵי חֲכָמִים בְּנַחַת נִשְׁמָעִים, *The gentle words of the wise are heard* (*Koheles* 9:17). Rav Pam had a very gentle manner of speaking. This was a primary reason why people were always ready to listen to what Rav Pam had to say.

In Rav Pam's last years, when illness made it very difficult for him to walk to shul, he had a minyan in his home on Shabbos. When a new *gabbai* called Rav Pam to the Torah, he said "*Ya'amod Moreinu* (our Guide) *HaRav Avraham Yaakov ben Meir HaKohen."* After davening, Rav Pam told the *gabbai* privately, "My father, *zichrono livrachah*, learned in Radin together with Reb Elchonon Wasserman; he later became a Rav and was a *maggid shiur* in Yeshivah Rabbeinu Chaim Berlin." The *gabbai* understood the message: Rav Pam's father should be referred to as "*HaRav* Meir."

As the *gabbai* recalls, "I never felt bad when Rav Pam offered criticism; he said it in such a way that you didn't feel bad."

Avoid Indictment

The *Zohar* teaches that what happens in *Shamayim* is a reflection of what happens on earth. When Jews speak well of each other, the Satan is silenced, but when Jews speak critically of each other, they give the Satan the "ammunition" he needs to stand before Hashem and prosecute *Klal Yisrael*.

Rav Pam was unusually careful never to speak critically of his fellow Jews. He was also extremely careful *not to listen* to anything which seemed to be critical of Jews.

Once, Rav Pam told a visitor a story that praised the ways of a certain rav in the previous generation. The visitor responded, "Ah, that's how it was by *amalig'e rabbanim* (rabbis of yesteryear) ..." which seemed to imply that there was a wide gap between them and today's rabbanim.

Rav Pam responded rather forcefully. "What do you mean? Today's *yungeleit* (young scholars) who can *pasken she'eilos* (offer halachic decisions) have nothing to be ashamed of, both in their amount of knowledge and their ability to apply it."

After Rav Pam underwent major surgery in 1997, he was visited at home by someone to whom he was very close. The man decided that rather than discuss important issues which might prove a strain for Rav Pam, he would speak about topics that would bring joy to him. He proceeded to tell Rav Pam a number of stories involving Jews who performed great acts of kindness in a hidden manner so that their deeds would not bring them any recognition. Rav Pam's joy was obvious. When the man had concluded his final story, Rav Pam said, "A father enjoys hearing good about his children. When you relate such wonderful stories about Yidden, the *Shechinah* comes to listen. I am confident that in this *zechus*, I will get well."

He always sought to see the good in others.

Once, a talmid was walking Rav Pam home from yeshivah when a middle-aged Russian woman stopped and tearfully asked for a *berachah* that her children should be religious Jews. When she had left, Rav Pam said, "*Ribono shel Olam*, look at this Russian woman; that her children should be *ehrliche Yidden* (upright Jews) — this is for what she yearns. *Mi ke'amcha Yisrael!*"

Powerful Words

Though he was amazingly humble, Rav Pam would readily grant *berachos* whenever asked to. Undoubtedly, this was in part because he was a *kohen* and *kohanim* have a special power of *berachah*. The teaching, "Do not make light of the blessing of a plain person" (*Megillah* 15a) may also have been a factor.

After his passing, a number of people came forward to relate how their hopes and dreams came true after receiving Rav Pam's *berachah*.

When a talmid decided to purchase a home, he sought and received his rebbi's *berachah*. A week and a half later, he found the house that was to become his home. The talmid firmly believes that this success was due to Rav Pam's *berachah*. The talmid told this to Rav Pam and related the following story:

> *Rabbi Yaakov Kamenetsky felt an eternal debt of gratitude toward the Wolpin family, whom he first met when he arrived in Seattle in 1938. Over the years he attended many Wolpin family simchos. As he left one bar mitzvah, Reb Yaakov was approached by the family's grandmother, Mrs. Kaila Wolpin. She thanked him for coming, to which he replied, "As they say in America, 'The pleasure is mine.'" Mrs. Wolpin then asked for a berachah. Reb Yaakov seemed to brush off the request by saying: "What do you mean? You will live as long as me!"*
>
> *Reb Yaakov passed away one day after his 95th birthday. Mrs. Wolpin passed away ten days after her 95th birthday.*

A great talmid chacham commented: Reb Yaakov's words, "You will live as long as me!" were not necessarily said with Ruach HaKodesh. Reb Yaakov symbolized emes, truth, and in that zechus, his words had special power.

Similarly, said Rav Pam's talmid, because Rav Pam was so incredibly careful with how he used his power of speech, therefore the berachos that he uttered were amazingly effective.

A Blessing for Nachas

Once, a renowned chassidic rebbe contacted a talmid of Rav Pam and made the follow request: The rebbe wanted an appointment with Rav Pam, but he wanted it to remain a private meeting, without his *gabba'im* accompanying him. He asked the young man to arrange such a meeting.

On the appointed day, the two were welcomed by Rav Pam into his modest home. Rav Pam led his honored guest up the stairs to his study, while the young man prepared to seat himself on a sofa downstairs. However, Rav Pam invited his talmid to join the rebbe and himself upstairs in his study.

After a bit of conversation, the rebbe explained the purpose of his visit. "As a rebbe of chassidim, I do not give my own children as much time as I would like to. I would like a *berachah* from the Rosh Yeshivah that I should be *matzliach* (successful) with my children." Rav Pam offered a warm, lengthy *berachah* which, as always, came straight from the heart.

CHAPTER NINE

Midos From Which We All Can Learn

In 1998, two of the great Torah leaders of our time, Rabbi Aharon Leib Steinman and the Gerrer Rebbe (Rabbi Yaakov Aryeh Alter), made their first joint visit to America. Together, they called on Rav Pam at his home. Later, Rav Pam met with Rav Steinman at the home of R' Avraham Biderman. These were the only times that the two ever met.

Later, Rav Steinman told Rabbi Nesanel Quinn,[1] "Rav Pam's

1. Rav Quinn served as Menahel of Mesivta Torah Vodaath for decades, and was admired as a great tzaddik.

Welcoming Rabbi Aharon Leib Steinman and the Gerrer Rebbe to his home

midos and sweetness are unusual." Rav Quinn responded, "I have known R' Avraham for close to 80 years and I can say that I have never seen him angry."

> *Once, Rav Pam spoke to a talmid concerning something wrong that the boy had done. "I see that Rebbi is angry at me," the talmid said. "Angry?" Rav Pam echoed. "No, I'm not angry; I love you. But I am unhappy over what you did."*

When Rav Pam would speak to talmidim about refining their *midos*, he would say, "It's not your nature, it's your choice," and he would quote Rambam as proof.[2] When a talmid asked him, "Did Rebbi have to work to learn how to control his *ka'as* (anger)?" Rav Pam replied, "Certainly."

2. *Hilchos Teshuvah* 5:1.

Sensitivity

When Rav Pam lived in East New York, he traveled by public transportation to the Torah Vodaath campus in Williamsburg. When riding the bus or train, Rav Pam never took a seat next to a student of the mesivta or beis midrash; he would sit next to boys of elementary school age. Rav Pam would ask the boy his name, grade, and what he was learning. He then would delight in speaking with the child about his studies.

One day, a talmid of Rav Pam who often traveled on the same bus to yeshivah asked him, "Why does Rebbi always sit next to the younger boys?" Rav Pam replied that, of course, he enjoyed speaking with older talmidim about what they were learning. However, he was concerned that this might make a mesivta or beis midrash student uncomfortable, because he would feel that Rav Pam was trying to test him. The elementary age children would not have such fears.

Once, Rav Pam fulfilled the mitzvah of nichum aveilim where he knew that one of the mourners was the mother of a talmid. Before leaving the house, he made a point of telling the mother that her son was an outstanding ben Torah. Later that day in yeshivah, another talmid approached Rav Pam and said, "Our family really appreciated the Rebbi's visit."

"Your family?" Rav Pam responded. "What do you mean?"

The talmid explained that his mother and the other bachur's mother were sisters.

Two months later, when attending a simchah, Rav Pam asked to be introduced to the second talmid's mother. "I must ask your forgiveness," he said. "I had no idea that you are ________'s mother." And he proceeded to tell her that her son was outstanding. The woman later confided to her son that indeed she had felt bad to hear her nephew praised and not her son. But Rav Pam's sensitivity took care of the problem.

One of Torah Vodaath's *tzedakah* projects is Keren Yitzchak Zvi,[3] which provides funding for Chinuch Atzmai schools in Eretz Yisrael. Each year, the yeshivah conducts a campaign on Purim to raise money for the fund. A few years ago, a certain talmid in the beis midrash agreed to direct the Purim campaign. It was not until later that this talmid joined Rav Pam's *shiur*, and until that Purim campaign, he had had very little personal contact with Rav Pam. However, during the three weeks leading up to Purim, he frequently consulted

At a Purim mesibah in Mesivta Torah Vodaath

3. Founded in memory of Yitzchok Zvi Perlman, a talmid of the yeshivah.

Rav Pam, who had been deeply involved with Keren Yitzchak Zvi since its founding.

After Purim, the talmid had a personal matter that he wanted to discuss with Rav Pam. He approached Rav Pam one morning after Shacharis and Rav Pam, still wrapped in his tallis and tefillin, led him to his office.

In the office, Rav Pam said apologetically, "I'm sorry, but I don't remember your name." This was not surprising, as throughout the three weeks of the campaign, the talmid had mentioned his name to Rav Pam only once. Nevertheless, it seems that Rav Pam felt bad about it, and wanted to make it up to the young man. After the talmid told him his name, Rav Pam said, "I want to tell you a joke, but first I must take off my tefillin." He removed his tefillin and said, "They say two things about old people: one is that they are forgetful; and the second thing ... I forgot!"

A talmid of Rav Pam who had been orphaned of his father became engaged and a wedding date was set. A few weeks

Embracing a talmid at his wedding

before the wedding, someone passed by this *chasan* in the Torah Vodaath beis midrash and inquired as to the Hebrew date of his wedding. When the *chasan* replied, the other bachur said, "What? You can't get married then! The *minhag* is not to make weddings on that night."

Actually, *some* conduct themselves according to this *minhag*; however, many do make weddings on that night. This *chasan* had never heard of this *minhag* and he had no way of knowing if his deceased father would have objected to his wedding date. His well-meaning friend had caused him to be overcome by a wave of panic. The *chasan* rushed through the beis midrash to where Rav Pam was sitting and blurted out his dilemma.

Rav Pam took his talmid's hand in his own. "What day is the wedding?" he asked kindly. The *chasan* told him the date. Rav Pam smiled broadly. "It will be a *very mazel'dig* day!" he declared. The *chasan's* spirits were restored.

Thoughtfulness

One Motza'ei Shabbos, as Rav Pam exited the beis midrash of Torah Vodaath following Maariv, he was met by someone who had driven there as soon as Shabbos had ended, to discuss a very important matter. "Can I drive the Rosh Yeshivah to his house?" the man asked. This was in Rav Pam's last years, when it was very important for his health that he walk a sizable distance each day. He had planned, therefore, to walk home. However, he told his visitor, "Yes, I will accept your offer for a ride — this way, you will not have to walk back to yeshivah to get your car."

At a wedding, Rav Pam was talking with a former talmid when another former talmid approached to ask if he could snap a picture of them. Rav Pam gladly obliged and then said to the photographer, "Most probably you would also like a picture of yourself with me?" Someone else held the camera as Rav Pam and his talmid posed together.

Examining the kesubah at a wedding

Once, when he was hospitalized during his final year, a family member read him a number of letters written by children from Shuvu. Later that day, a grandchild came to visit and, noticing the pile of letters, picked them up and read them aloud. Rav Pam reacted to each letter as if he was hearing it for the first time, to make his grandchild happy.

When a *sofer* completed the checking of the mezuzos in Rav Pam's house, Rav Pam paid the *sofer* and then called the *sofer's* assistant aside. "Thank you very much for your assistance," he said, as he placed an envelope containing a tip into the young man's pocket.

> *One day, Rav Pam was standing outside his home with a talmid. They were engaged in Torah discussion as the talmid's young children played with each other. Suddenly, Rav Pam turned to the children and said, "How does a person talk? Like this, like the way I am talking to you. And how does a dog talk? By barking. That is its way of talking.*

"Now, next door to my house there is a dog. Most probably it is soon going to bark. But don't be afraid; that's just the way it talks."

A Thoughtful Expense

For the wedding of his son, R' Asher, Rav Pam hired the band to play until 11:30 P.M. At 11:29, the Lakewood Rosh Yeshivah, Rabbi Shneur Kotler, entered the wedding hall, and moments later the music stopped. Rav Pam sent someone to the band leader and asked that the band play for an additional half-hour for which he would, of course, pay overtime charges. The band leader was very apologetic. "Please tell Rabbi Pam that according to union regulations, overtime has to be paid by the hour; if we don't get paid for a full hour, we can't play at all." Rav Pam said that he would pay for the hour.

Rabbi Shneur Kotler dancing at the wedding of R' Asher Pam

The music started again and R' Shneur danced for a few minutes, wished "*Mazel tov,*" and left. The band played for the remaining time while the hall was almost empty, with no one dancing. Even the immediate families were ready to leave the hall well before the hour was over. Someone asked Rav Pam why he so readily agreed to such an expense for a few minutes of dancing. To Rav Pam, the answer was obvious. "What do you mean?" he replied. "Reb Shneur went to four weddings tonight. It required a great effort on his part to come here. Is it right that he should feel that he came for nothing?"

Room in His Heart

A young woman, a *giyores* (convert) living in Brooklyn, looked to Rav Pam as her guide and would turn to him with halachah questions. One day, she received a phone call that her grandfather, who lived in New Jersey, had died. She decided on her own that although she was Jewish and her grandfather was a non-Jew, it would be proper for her to attend the funeral, which would be held in a funeral home. She would not attend the ceremony that would take place in a church.

In the funeral home, she was dismayed when the family began a Christian prayer service; she had thought that this would take place in the church. When the funeral was over, she left the building feeling very bad and very alone.

When she reached the George Washington Bridge, she went to a pay phone and called Rav Pam. She told him what had happened and expressed her feelings to him. Rav Pam assured her that she had done nothing wrong; his words calmed her. He then asked, "So what's doing with *shidduchim* (marriage possibilities)?" The woman was amazed. Rav Pam, who was such a busy, sought-after person, cared enough about her to ask such a question!

She discussed her *shidduch* possibilities with Rav Pam for but a few minutes, but that short phone call transformed her mood from sadness to joy. She now realized that she was not alone at all. Rather, she was part of a very special nation, led by tzaddikim who have place in their hearts for everyone's troubles.

Sharing the Burden

The quality of נוֹשֵׂא בְּעוֹל עִם חֲבֵרוֹ, to feel the suffering of other Jews in a way that makes their burden easier to bear, is a most important *midah*. By doing this, we truly make the other person feel better, for he knows that there is someone who cares about him and is taking his troubles to heart.

When a little boy was diagnosed with a terrible disease, his father visited Rav Pam. The father had never learned in Torah Vodaath and had little contact with Rav Pam until that time, but he knew that Rav Pam was a tzaddik who cared deeply for everyone.

He handed Rav Pam a large sum to distribute to *tzedakah* and a slip of paper with his son's name, and he asked that Rav Pam *daven* for the child. Six weeks later, when the father returned, Rav Pam asked him, "How is Yisrael ben ________?" Just knowing that Rav Pam knew their son's name by heart because he had been davening for him for the past six weeks was a great source of strength to both father and mother.

Six months later, as the boy continued to undergo difficult treatments, the family's rav came to Rav Pam and said, "The family requested that the Rosh Yeshivah continue to have the boy in mind." Rav Pam replied sincerely, "I don't know what else to do — I *daven* for him three times a day."

Davening at his seat in the Torah Vodaath beis midrash

When Rav Pam was informed that the boy had responded to the treatments and was doing well, his joy was indescribable.

Gratitude

The trait of *hakaras hatov* (gratitude) is basic to proper service of Hashem. *Sefer HaChinuch* writes that this trait is the reason for the mitzvah to honor our parents, and that by feeling gratitude towards our parents, we will come to feel gratitude towards Hashem.

Nothing that anyone did for Rav Pam went unnoticed. As Rabbi Elya Svei put it, "If anyone did a kindness for him, or for one of his children or grandchildren ... the Rosh Yeshivah [Rav Pam] felt that there was no way he could repay it. He would do everything that he possibly could for that person."

At an Agudath Israel convention:
Rabbi Moshe Sherer, Rav Pam, the Novominsker Rebbe

Rav Pam always made sure to express his appreciation, and sometimes he did this long after the favor had been done.

In his last years when he was ill, a minyan would daven in his home on Shabbos and Yom Tov. One Rosh Hashanah, he asked the *baal tokei'a* (person who blows the shofar) to try to sound each *tekiah* longer than the accepted norm. The *baal tokei'ah* obliged and performed the mitzvah very well. When he finished, Rav Pam said that the the *tekios* had "filled him with *simchah* (happiness)." Three weeks later, at the festive gathering in his home on Shemini Atzeres, Rav Pam told the person, "I still think about those *tekios*!"

Before leaving conventions of Agudath Israel or Torah Umesorah, Rav Pam made sure to go to the kitchen and thank the cooks.

In the early 1970s, Rav Pam, then a rebbi in the Torah Vodaath beis midrash, was invited to become Rosh Yeshivah of

Rav Pam's only visit to Eretz Yisrael was in the summer of 1971. He spent one week of his trip at the Ponovezh Yeshivah yarchei kallah in Bnei Brak, where he did what he enjoyed most — learning Torah. In this photograph, Rav Pam (at shtender) is attending a shiur in the main beis midrash of Ponovezh.

a highly regarded kollel in Eretz Yisrael and its newly founded beis midrash. He was offered a substantial salary. Rav Pam declined the offer almost immediately. When his son asked why, he replied, "How can I leave Torah Vodaath? I owe so much to the yeshivah! I learned here, the yeshivah gave me a position when I needed one ..."

A Special Notebook

As a rule, Rav Pam did not accept gifts and he tried to avoid accepting favors from others. He usually made his own arrangements for transportation to *simchas*, saying that he found it easier this way. If he needed to go somewhere for personal reasons, he preferred the bus or subway rather than having someone drive him. At age 75, he traveled by subway to the Lower East Side to fulfill the mitzvah of *nichum aveilim* (comforting mourners). He would not allow anyone to drive him there.

For many years, Mrs. Miller was the woman behind the counter at the corner grocery, serving the talmidim of Torah Vodaath and other neighborhood customers. Whenever she noticed Rav Pam on line waiting to be served, she would call out, "Please, Rav Pam, come to the front of the line!" He would always politely refuse, saying that he would wait his turn. Of course, the *bachurim* ahead of him on line had already asked that he go ahead of them and they had received the same response.

When, on occasion, Rav Pam did accept a favor, he felt indebted to the person. He therefore had a special notebook in which he would record information which he could use to "return the favor." "So-and-so gave me a ride today. He has a 21-year-old daughter in need of a *shidduch*."

Gratitude Amid Pain

During the last five years of his life, when he was ill and often in pain, Rav Pam never bemoaned his situation or uttered the slightest complaint. At a *seudas hoda'ah* (meal of thanksgiving) held two years before his passing for a relative who had recovered from a serious car accident, Rav Pam said:

> *A seudas hoda'ah is a time for all the participants to reflect on the gratitude which they owe Hashem Yisbarach. I myself know how much appreciation I owe Hashem for all that He does for me. We should be ashamed of ourselves to complain over small problems when we have so much for which to be grateful.*

Rav Pam descends the stairs to participate in a meeting held in his dining room.

Each week, at the conclusion of Mussaf in his home, Rav Pam would publicly thank the *baalei tefillah*, the *baal korei* and all those who had come to be part of his minyan. Rav Pam was thanking everyone when, in fact, everyone felt it a great privilege to be a part of Rav Pam's minyan and to have the opportunity of observing this tzaddik from close up.

During davening, Rav Pam would sit at the head of his dining room table, while others occupied the remaining chairs. Other people sat in the adjoining living room, while some people stood. One Shabbos, two men were motioning to each other to sit in the only remaining empty chair. Then they noticed Rav Pam, stooped over and weak, going into the kitchen and dragging a chair towards the dining room so that both of them could sit. They quickly hurried over and took the chair themselves.

Another time, one man went and brought a chair for a second man. Later, Rav Pam told the man, "Thank you for bringing the chair. Really, it's my responsibility to see that everyone has a place to sit, so I appreciate that you brought the chair."

During hospital stays as he struggled with his illness, Rav Pam never gave any indication that he was in pain, even at times when the tests being administered were clearly painful. What he *did* show was the gratitude that he felt toward the doctors and nurses who tended to him. He would thank the hospital staff for anything, large or small, that was done for him.

Years earlier, when he was hospitalized for a short time, a nurse told someone, "Rabbi Pam was our easiest patient; he never needed anything."

His Love of Children

During the summer of Rav and Rebbetzin Pam's engagement, Rav Pam and his parents spent some time vacationing in the Catskill Mountains. When Rav Pam would take a break from his learning schedule to go for a walk in the fresh country air, he would take along a boy of about six. Every day at the same time, the two would walk to the top of a hill, from

With a talmid's children

where they would watch a train go by. For Rav Pam, a walk in the country was an opportunity to make a young child happy.

For a number of years, the Russel family lived in Kensington on the same block as the Pams. In the summer, their young children would wait outside, along with other children their age, for the morning day camp bus. As Rav Pam would pass the little boys, he would wish them a hearty "Good morning," and sometimes, he gave each one a kiss. As he passed the little girls, they would respectfully move back to allow Rav Pam to pass, but he would say, "No, bnos Yisrael, you stay where you are," and he would step off the sidewalk and walk around them.

Camera-Ready

When an eight-year-old boy heard that Rav Pam was visiting someone in Far Rockaway, he ran to get his camera and waited outside the house. As the door opened and Rav Pam emerged at the top of the steps, the boy raised his camera. "One moment," said a smiling Rav Pam. He adjusted his hat, straightened his tie and posed for the picture. Then, he descended the stairs and extended his hand in greeting to the boy and to a friend who was with him. He then asked the boys their names. "Avrohom Bender," the child with the camera replied. "I know your father and I knew your grandfather," Rav Pam told the boy. The other boy said that his name was Yair. " 'Yair' means to light up," Rav Pam told him. "You will light up the world!"

Once, three young boys decided that it would be a good idea to wake up early and snap some pictures of Rav Pam as he walked to yeshivah for Shacharis. They met him outside his house. The boys took turns; one boy spoke to Rav Pam as they walked, while the other two took pictures.

Posing for an eight-year-old photographer

Rav Pam did not seem to mind at all; he acted in a wholly natural way, as if there was no camera in front of him. When they entered the yeshivah building, he asked the boys, "Do you still have some more pictures to take?" The boys assured him that they had finished and Rav Pam then went to daven.

To Make a Child Happy

Rav Pam once asked a boy, "What is your name?" "Shlomo Baruch," the boy replied. "Do you know where your full name appears in *Tanach*?" asked Rav Pam. Without waiting for a reply, Rav Pam got a *Tanach* and showed the boy the *pasuk*: וְהַמֶּלֶךְ שְׁלֹמֹה בָּרוּךְ, *For King Shlomo is blessed* (*I Melachim* 2:45). That boy never forgot this brief encounter.

A former talmid came to ask Rav Pam where to send his son, an eighth grader, for high school.

The father was leaning towards Torah Vodaath, but was concerned that his son did not know anyone in the yeshivah and would feel lost. "That's not a problem," Rav Pam said. "You know that he can find me in the beis midrash. Tell him to come to me every day; I'll give him a knip (pinch on the cheek) and a pat on the back."

Once, a ten-year-old child who had come to daven Shacharis in Torah Vodaath seated himself at a *shtender* (lectern) in the center of the beis midrash, not realizing that he had taken Rav Pam's seat. As Rav Pam entered, wrapped in tallis and tefillin, several older talmidim went over to the child to ask him to move. Rav Pam, however, called the boy back, moved his tallis bag to one side of the wide, low shtender and shared his seat with the child.

Berachos for All

At a Torah Umesorah convention, Rav Pam spoke of the great *zechus* (merit) of devoting one's life to learning and teaching Torah. A young man attending the convention was very moved by Rav Pam's words. He wanted to bring his little boy (whom he had brought along) to Rav Pam for a *berachah*, but not having had any previous contact with Rav Pam, he was hesitant to do so.

The young man approached a friend whom Rav Pam knew well, and said, "If you can arrange for my son to get a *berachah* from Rav Pam, I'll do my best to have my son devote his life to Torah." Arrangements were made; father and son were brought to Rav Pam, who bestowed upon the little boy a very heartfelt and beautiful

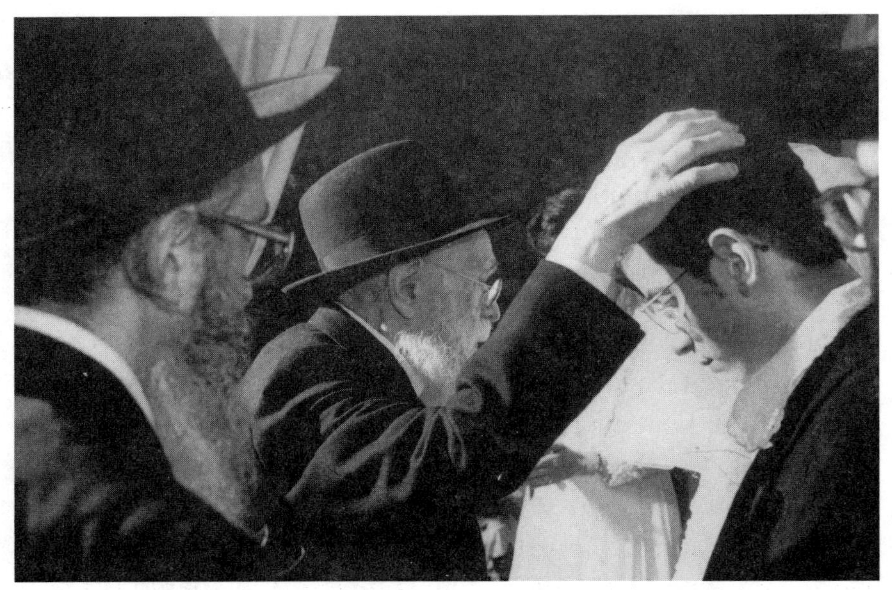

Rav Pam confers his berachah at his grandson's chuppah

berachah. Then Rav Pam turned to the father and said, "But what about your daughter? — she also deserves a *berachah*!"

The young man was astounded. When he and his family had arrived at the hotel for the convention, they had passed Rav Pam on the staircase. Rav Pam had remembered that the family included a little girl — and he wanted to make sure that she too received a *berachah*. The grateful father hurried to find his daughter. When she stood before Rav Pam, he blessed her that she should grow to become a true *bas Yisrael* and marry a true *ben Torah*. This *berachah* has already been fulfilled.

Pesach Gets His Chance

One of Rav Pam's close talmidim was a "regular" at the Shabbos minyan in Rav Pam's home during his final years. The talmid's six-year-old son, Pesach, wanted very much to accompany his father to the minyan, but for a long time his father resisted, for he felt that the 40-minute walk was too long for the boy and that he would not be able to sit quietly for the entire davening.

However, on the last day of Pesach, only a few months before Rav Pam passed away, the little boy got his chance. His father recalled the deep impression it had made on him when *his* father had taken him to see a tzaddik, so he decided to allow Pesach to come along.

He seated Pesach next to himself and the boy sat quietly throughout the *tefillos*. As a reward for his good behavior, Pesach was brought to Rav Pam's side after davening had ended and everyone else had left. Rav Pam asked the little boy his name and then said: "You know, Pesach, I was so proud of you. I watched you daven and you sat there so nicely. Welcome to our minyan — you can come whenever you want!"

Rav Pam continued, "Pesach, are you *b'simchah* (happy)?" The boy nodded. "Who is your rebbi?" The boy named a rebbi at Yeshivah Torah Vodaath. "Oh, he's a great rebbi!" Rav Pam exclaimed. "But make sure that you are happy when you are learning — you should always be *b'simchah*!"

"... And, you know, Pesach, I have the same problem that you have ... My glasses slip down my nose, too," he explained. The elderly tzaddik and the little boy looked at each other and, in unison, pushed their glasses higher up.

Forever Striving

Rav Pam once revealed to someone that he kept in his pocket a paper on which he had written a famous statement of the Vilna *Gaon*:

עִיקָר עֲבוֹדַת הָאָדָם בָּעוֹלָם הַזֶּה הוּא לְתַקֵּן הַמִּדוֹת.

Man's main purpose in this world is to correct his midos.

He explained why he had this paper. "It's worthwhile to review this statement of the *Gra*, to see it again and again, for every time one sees it and reviews it, it brings new *chizuk* (strengthening of spirit)."

Rav Pam said this approximately 18 months before he passed away. Even at that point in his life, he felt that he needed *chizuk*, so that he would continue to perfect his *midos*.

What should *we* say?

CHAPTER TEN

A Path of Peace

Rabbi Yosef Elias knew Rav Pam for over half a century. He said that whenever he discussed something important with Rav Pam, he learned the lesson of דִּבְרֵי חֲכָמִים בְּנַחַת נִשְׁמָעִים, *The gentle words of the wise are heard (Koheles* 9:17). Rav Pam never raised his voice, always spoke respectfully, and always followed the path of peace. He stayed away from *machlokes* (dispute) as from a fire.

Once, a group visited Rav Pam to ask that he become involved in a dispute. After his polite refusals were not accepted, Rav

At a family simchah: (left to right) Rabbi Aharon Pam, Rav Pam, Rabbi Yosef Elias

Pam finally said, "All my life I toiled not to become involved in *machlokes*. This required tremendous effort and skill. And now you want to pull me into this mud? I'm sorry, this will not happen."

A Time to Forgive

A certain young man was terribly mistreated by a neighbor, who made his life miserable. Before Yom Kippur, the young man asked a rav if he had to be *mochel* (forgive) this man. The rav replied that as long as the neighbor did not ask for forgiveness, he was not required to be *mochel*. But when the young man asked Rav Pam the same question, he received a different response. "Be *mochel* him," said Rav Pam. "We also do things wrong, yet we want Hashem to be *mochel* us. To be *mochel* others is a *zechus* that helps us to gain forgiveness from Hashem."

A Time to Seek Forgiveness

It happened that a man involved with a certain yeshivah had an excellent idea through which large sums of money could be raised for that yeshivah. But when he suggested the idea, a certain individual vetoed the suggestion. Since Rav Pam was involved with this yeshivah, the man called Rav Pam and asked that he convince the other person to retract his veto; otherwise, the idea would never get off the ground. Rav Pam replied that, unfortunately, he could not get involved, and the idea never got off the ground.

Half a year later, shortly before Rosh Hashanah, this man received a letter from Rav Pam, asking his forgiveness in case this episode had caused him distress. The man was astounded that Rav Pam recalled this incident after so many months had passed. He was also impressed that Rav Pam had realized that the incident might have upset him, which it did.

The man wrote back to Rav Pam thanking him for his letter and assuring him that while he had been distressed, it was not Rav Pam who had caused it.

"Seek an Alternative"

A former talmid, Aryeh Gross,[1] was on the verge of registering his son in a certain yeshivah. Before any agreements were made, Aryeh received a phone call from an angry relative. The relative had had an unpleasant experience with that yeshivah and he was shocked when he learned that Aryeh was on the verge of registering his son there for the coming school year.

---

1. Not his real name.

Aryeh calmly replied that while he sympathized with his relative for the unpleasant experience which he had been through, he did not see how this affected *him*. But his relative saw things differently. To his mind, for Aryeh to associate himself with that yeshivah was a slap in the face to *him*.

Over the next couple of weeks, Aryeh received many phone calls from this individual, each call more furious than the previous one. Finally, the relative told him, "If you register your son in that yeshivah, I and my family will have nothing to do with you."

"My decision is final," was Aryeh's reply.

A few days later, Aryeh met Rav Pam, who had received a phone call from the relative. "I was shocked by the conversation," Rav Pam said. "It was astounding." Aryeh was certain that his rebbi was astonished at how unreasonable his relative was being. He was certain that Rav Pam would tell him to ignore any further phone calls from this man.

How astounded he was by Rav Pam's next words. "I was shocked to see how deeply sensitive a human being can be!" True, the man was being unreasonable, but that was because he felt so hurt at whatever had transpired between himself and that yeshivah. It was because he was so hurt that he was so angry and threatening. Rav Pam, with his own deep sensitivity, saw past the man's angry words. He recognized the pain that the man was feeling in his heart.

"I would advise you," continued Rav Pam, "to seek an alternative. Try to find another yeshivah that would be suitable for your son. If you do seek an alternative and nothing works out, at least you will be able to tell your relative that you tried.

"You will see," he concluded, "that by doing this, you will have *hatzlachah* (success)."

Aryeh followed his rebbi's advice. In the end, he registered his son in another yeshivah. One year later, he told Rav Pam, "Rebbi cannot imagine how much his advice to be *rodeph shalom* (pursue peace) has been blessed with *hatzlachah.*" Upon hearing these words, Rav Pam wept tears of joy.

Shalom Bayis

A newly married couple was having a serious disagreement. The husband, a fine *ben Torah*, insisted that he wanted to live like the Chofetz Chaim. All he needed was a plain table, a couple of chairs that did not have to match, some shelves for *sefarim* and dishes, and the plainest, used bedroom furniture. His wife, a fine, modest *bas Yisrael*, was not interested in lavish furnishings, but she was not satisfied with a "Chofetz

Chaim-style" home. She wanted the standard type of furniture found in a typical, middle-class Jewish home of the time.

The husband had never learned in Torah Vodaath and had no previous contact with Rav Pam. However, he knew that Rav Pam had a reputation for great success in restoring *shalom bayis*, peace between husband and wife. He called Rav Pam and asked if he and his wife could come visit him in his home.

The couple sat with Rav Pam and explained their problem. Rav Pam then spoke to each one separately. To the husband, he said that the Chofetz Chaim was unique even in his generation for the amazingly simple life that he lived. He was the exception, not the rule. Surely, then, in America today where the average family has a far nicer home than people had in Poland 70 years ago, a wife cannot be expected to live as the Chofetz Chaim lived.

To the wife, Rav Pam spoke words of *chizuk*, as a way of erasing any hard feelings that may have been caused by the disagreement she and her husband had been having.

Today, many years later, this couple are proud grandparents, and enjoy a life of Torah and *shalom bayis*. And they credit this to Rav Pam.

Dancing at a simchah in the dining room of Mesivta Torah Vodaath

A Tzaddik's Home

The mutual respect, devotion and consideration which Rav Pam and his rebbetzin had for one another was obvious to all.

Once, a talmid arranged to stay in the Torah Vodaath dormitory over Rosh Hashanah. On Erev Yom Tov, he asked his rebbi, Rav Pam, if he could eat one of the Yom Tov meals at his home. Rav Pam replied, "That is my rebbetzin's department. I will ask her and let you know."

That night, when the bachur wished his rebbi "*Gut Yom Tov*," Rav Pam said, "It would be our pleasure to have you join us for a *seudah*. Normally, I would have told you that right away. But my rebbetzin had a hard week and I did not feel that it was right for me to invite a guest without first asking her."

A talmid who studied in kollel while his wife held a full-time job asked him, "Is there anything wrong with my preparing some of the Shabbos foods to help my wife? A friend of mine felt that it was not the right thing for a man to do."

At the sheva berachos seudah of his son R' Dovid

Rav Pam replied, "All the years that my wife worked in the public school system and came home late on Fridays, I would prepare the kugel."

For many years, talmidim noticed that, upon arriving at yeshivah Shabbos morning for davening, Rav Pam would first go the women's

Rabbi Shlomo Heiman

section to prepare a *siddur* and *chumash* for his rebbetzin, who would be arriving later.

Rav Pam related that he learned many lessons in good *midos*, especially how to honor one's wife, from Rabbi Shlomo Heiman, who served as Rosh Yeshivah of Torah Vodaath from 1935 until 1944.

When a doctor informed R' Shlomo that he could no longer have salt in his diet, the rosh yeshivah turned to his wife and asked with a smile, "Do you think that it is possible for you to cook food that is *un taam* (tasteless)?" In this way, R' Shlomo used the opportunity to compliment his wife on her cooking skills.

In His Last Years

When, due to illness, he began to daven at home on Shabbos and Yom Tov, some who were close to Rav Pam urged him to allow a *minyan* to daven with him. For a long time he resisted, because he felt it was unfair to confine the Rebbetzin to the second floor of their house. He finally accepted the suggestion when the Rebbetzin said that the idea of a *minyan* was a very good one and that she would be able to come into the kitchen during davening by walking out the front door and coming back inside through the rear entrance.

It happened one Shabbos that the streets were covered with snow and salt, and much of it was tracked into Rav Pam's home by the many who came to daven. By the time Shabbos was over, the floor was terribly dirty. On Motza'ei Shabbos, the doorbell rang. Rebbetzin Pam opened the door to find a former talmid of Rav Pam, and his son, standing there. They had davened with the minyan on Shabbos.

"We came to wash the floor," the young man said. At first, Rebbetzin Pam was taken aback by the offer. However, the young man was persistent and the floor did need a thorough cleaning. Rebbetzin Pam left the matter for her husband to decide. Rav Pam had two questions for his talmid. "Does your wife know that you are here?" and "Did you finish helping out at home?" Only after the talmid answered "Yes" to both questions did Rav Pam allow him to wash the floor.

On the last Purim of his life, the line of those who came to bring mishloach manos and greet him stretched from his dining room into the street. Rav Pam's face shone with the joy of Purim and the pleasure of seeing so many talmidim and others who felt close to him. Amid the tumult, he said to

Rav Pam with a Purim visitor

one visitor, "Please bring your little boy into the kitchen; I think my rebbetzin would enjoy seeing his costume."

One day, he was feeling very ill and needed to be taken to the hospital. A grandson happened to be with him and was to accompany him in the ambulance. As he was being wheeled out of the house, Rav Pam turned to his grandson and said, "Call your wife and tell her that you might be home late." This was in the afternoon and his grandson was not expected home for a while. But Rav Pam, though very ill and in pain, was thinking about the fact that his grandson's wife might later worry if her husband did not arrive home when expected.

This was Rav Pam, always thinking about others. It is no wonder that his home was a model of peace and harmony.

CHAPTER ELEVEN

Truth

It happened during Rav Pam's years as a mesivta rebbi. One morning, he began class by saying:

This morning in the subway station, the woman in the token booth showed me a student transportation pass and said, "This pass was confiscated because it was being used improperly. Do you work for this school?" and she pointed to the name of a yeshivah on the pass.

I replied that, no, I did not teach in that yeshivah, to which she responded, "Aren't you glad?"

"We learn two important lessons from this incident," Rav Pam told his talmidim. "First of all, a transportation pass should never be used improperly. Secondly, even a non-Jew understands that one should be 'glad' not to be associated with a place where some people do things that are dishonest.

"And how should one feel if, *chas v'shalom*, he *is* associated with such a place ... ?"

When teaching his talmidim and his own children about honesty, Rav Pam would speak of his dear friend, Rabbi Eliyahu Moshe Shisgal:

Shopping for *arba'ah minim* before Succos can be a difficult and tiring task. It is common to find customers examining dozens of *lulavim* in search of one that they will deem satisfactory. As a tzaddik who was extremely careful in his performance of mitzvos, Rav Shisgal surely wanted a *lulav* of the highest quality. Yet he would never pick up a *lulav* in a store unless it was handed to him by the storekeeper, for fear that if he himself were to lift it out of the box, he might accidently damage it and cause the storekeeper a loss.

If, while shopping, someone would ask Rav Shisgal whether a particular *esrog* or *lulav* was satisfactory by his standards, he would not respond. He was concerned that if he indicated he would not use the item, people might say that the merchandise was of poor quality.

Rav Pam had a different practice when shopping for *lulavim*. He would pick up a *lulav* to examine it, without the storekeeper's assistance. However, when paying for his *lulav* and *esrog*, he would add a few dollars, in case he had inadvertently damaged a *lulav*.

Honest with Himself

A talmid related:

Twenty years ago, when I first became a talmid of Rav Pam, an incident took place on a Simchas Torah night in yeshivah. There was a halachah that I needed to know for the next day. At a break in the hakafos, I asked Rav Pam my question. He replied that the question had been addressed by the Netziv[1] in his Sefer Meishiv Davar. At first, Rav Pam could not recall what the Netziv said about it. The sefer was then out of print, and not available in the yeshivah.

After a few minutes, his face lit up. He remembered the Netziv's ruling and the source upon which it was based. I was certainly satisfied and returned to the dancing.

A little while later, as I was dancing, I felt a tap on my shoulder. It was Rav Pam. "Do you have a raincoat? Come. I have the Sefer Meishiv Davar at home. Let's look up the teshuvah [the Netziv's discussion of the matter]."

I was surprised and very excited to have the opportunity for such a close personal experience. I rushed to get my coat.

As we were leaving, Rabbi Avraham Talansky, a member of the yeshivah administration, approached us. He had heard of my question. He

1. Rabbi Naftali Tzvi Yehudah Berlin, who headed the Volozhiner Yeshivah in the late 19th century.

told us that Rabbi Yaakov Kamenetsky had been asked the question and had responded in the same manner as Rav Pam.

My heart sank. I thought our walk home was lost. Why should Rav Pam go home in the rain and study the teshuvah, when he had already heard that R' Yaakov had said exactly what he had told me?

Rav Pam politely thanked Rabbi Talansky and then, together, we went to his home, where we learned through the teshuvah. It was just as he had said. We learned through two other teshuvos before heading back to yeshivah.

It was a wonderful experience, but quite unusual. During the walk back to yeshivah, I gently asked Rav Pam what had prompted him to walk home during hakafos. Was he unsure if he had remembered the teshuvah correctly?

Rav Pam answered that the dormitory students had visited his home that afternoon for a simchas Yom Tov (Yom Tov celebration). Rav Pam had spoken about dedication to learning, and in particular had mentioned Reb Zalman of Volozhin's self-sacrifice in traveling a considerable distance to look up a teshuvah.

He explained, "Initially, I could not remember the teshuvah. It disturbed me that at that moment, I didn't plan to go home to check the teshuvah. I had just spoken about this! This is why I had to walk home to check the sefer.

"A person must always be honest with himself."

It is difficult for me to express the impression that this conversation had on me. It was a private moment on a quiet street, as we walked in the rain. Rav Pam spoke very seriously, as if to impress upon me the importance he attached to this trip.

Impartial Judge

The Mishnah warns a judge to remain totally impartial when deciding a *din Torah*: "Do not act as a lawyer [by advising

one party as to how he should present his case]; while the parties stand before you, consider them both as guilty [so that you can remain fair and honest]; but when they are dismissed before you, consider them both as innocent, provided they have both accepted the judgment" (*Avos* 1:8).

Years ago, Rabbi Yaakov Kamenetsky asked Rav Pam to preside over a dispute between two yeshivos. On the appointed day, two distinguished representatives of one of the yeshivos entered the beis midrash of Mesivta Torah Vodaath and went directly to where Rav Pam sat. Rav Pam looked up from his *sefer*, recognized the two men but did not so much as nod towards them. He simply closed his *sefer*, stood up and led them out of the beis midrash.

A few minutes later, the other party, two men who appeared much younger than the first pair, entered the beis midrash looking for Rav Pam. A talmid of Rav Pam told them that his rebbi had left a few minutes earlier with some visitors. The two men were dismayed. "They got here first? They will use the opportunity to present their side and influence the Rosh Yeshivah!"

The talmid assured them that this would not happen. "I am certain that they will not influence my rebbi. In fact, I do not think that he even allowed them to speak with him before you arrived." He was right.

Man of His Word

In Rav Pam's last years, two men had a 10:00 A.M. appointment in his home to discuss an important matter. They rang the bell and were told that Rav Pam was in great pain and had not slept the entire night. They returned to their car and were about to drive away when Rabbi Dovid Pam, who was visiting his father, came running towards the car. His father wanted to see them. They entered the house to find Rav Pam descending the steps to the ground floor, appearing pale and alarmingly weak. He said to them, "I did not call to cancel the appointment, therefore I have no right to cancel it now."

He once told his son, R' Asher: "By us, a word is a contract."

His talmidim learned well the lesson of honoring one's word. A talmid who needed construction done in his home called two contractors for estimates. Some time passed, during which one contractor called back with a price, while the other one did not. The talmid grew tired of waiting and hired the man who had called back. An hour later, the other contractor called with a price that was several thousand dollars lower than the first price. The talmid immediately called Rav Pam, who said that he must honor his word and use the first contractor.

Correcting a Mistake

In the winter of 5761 (2001), on a Shabbos afternoon at Minchah, the chazzan of Rav Pam's minyan made a mistake during *chazaras hashatz*. Rav Pam, extremely weak and on strong medication, did not hear the mistake. When it was reported to him, he said that the chazzan should repeat the *berachah*. After davening was over and everyone had left, Rav Pam realized that according to the halachah, there was in fact no need to repeat the *berachah*.

The following night, a member of the *minyan* found a number of urgent messages on his cell phone from Rav Pam. When the man returned the call, Rav Pam informed him that he was calling regarding the incident at Minchah. On Motza'ei Shabbos, following the conclusion of Maariv, Rav Pam had announced to the minyan that he had erred and he stated the actual halachah. However, he later remembered that this man had been present for Minchah but not for Maariv. "I did not want an error in halachah to go forth from my home. Do you recall who else was at the minyan yesterday?" The man recalled that a neighbor had also been there for Minchah but not for Maariv, and he assured Rav Pam that he would call him and inform him of the correction. "Please say that I asked that you call," Rav Pam requested.

The following Shabbos, when the neighbor walked into the house for Minchah, Rav Pam immediately asked him, "Did you get the message about the mistake last week?"

His Responsibility

One of Rav Pam's talmidim is treasurer of a free-loan fund. Every so often, Rav Pam would call him to say that he had advised a certain individual to request a loan. That recommendation was, of course, sufficient for the talmid to grant the loan. In every such instance, Rav Pam would find out from the borrower when the loan was due and call a few days after the due date to see if the loan had been paid. "It is not necessary for Rebbi to call," the treasurer would say. After all, Rav Pam had not taken responsibility for the loan, he had merely given a recommendation. Nevertheless, Rav Pam felt personally responsible since the loan had been granted because of his recommendation. If the loan was not paid, then within a few days Rav Pam himself would pay the loan in full.

Lessons in Honesty

One year, New York was struck by a major snowstorm. How surprised the talmidim were on the morning of the storm when Rav Pam, who had to travel quite a distance, arrived in yeshivah on time! One talmid remarked to another, "Knowing that it would take longer to get here, Rebbi left his house extra early." It was a lesson that the talmidim would never forget.

One stormy winter day, someone entered the office of a Brooklyn notary public. (A notary public has the legal power to notarize documents, meaning, to bear witness that he has witnessed others sign such documents.) The client had in his possession a document that was to be signed by himself and Rav Pam and which had to be notarized. The notary, an Orthodox Jew, always had the person sign the document in his presence

Arriving at a Shuvu dinner in a snowstorm

as the law requires. However, Rav Pam was not present and could not be expected to venture outside in such weather. The notary decided to make an exception this one time. He told the person, "You sign in my presence and make sure that Rav Pam signs it today as well." After the client signed, the notary affixed his stamp and signature to the document.

Later, the notary was astounded when the door of his office opened and in walked Rav Pam. "Your stamp reads, 'Signed before me,'" he said simply. Rav Pam then signed his name in the notary's presence, thanked the man and left.

A Mug on the Edge

In the hallway outside the offices of the Torah Vodaath *hanhalah* (administration) stood a closet which was there for the *hanhalah* members to use. A student in the beis midrash kept a coffee mug on a shelf in that closet. One day, he placed the mug very close to the shelf's edge. When Rav Pam opened the closet door to hang up his coat before Shacharis, the mug fell to the floor and broke. Rav Pam asked a student standing nearby to show

him where a broom and dustpan could be found. He insisted on sweeping up the pieces himself. After Shacharis, he told the talmidim who had lined up to speak with him that he had to attend to something and would not be available until later. A talmid followed him and watched as he went to a nearby hardware store (which had a mikveh for utensils) to purchase a new mug, which he later placed where the original mug had been kept. He left the following note (written in Hebrew) inside the mug:

> *To the owner of the mug: Pashati — I was negligent and broke your mug. I bought you a new one to replace it. If you are not satisfied with the new one, or if you want money instead, please let me know.*
>
> A. Pam

In the last four and a half years of his life, Rav Pam's ill health often made it impossible for him to deliver his *Yoreh De'ah shiur*. At one point, he had to be convinced to accept his salary check, for he argued that he was entitled to it only if he was earning it! It was this thought, coupled with his incredible devotion to his talmidim, that impelled Rav Pam to say the *shiur* in his dining room, with talmidim crowded around his table, whenever possible.

Cause for a Relapse

In the summer of 1992, after having developed high blood pressure, Rav Pam was recovering from its effects and was feeling better. One evening, however, his blood pressure rose and he did not feel well. He told someone that he knew what had caused his relapse.

That evening, he had been *mesader kiddushin* at a chuppah ceremony that had been scheduled to take place before sunset. Arrangements had been made for a car to pick him up at his home, but for some reason, the car never arrived. Rav Pam called a car service and a few minutes later, a car pulled up. After entering the car, Rav Pam realized that, in fact, it had been summoned by a neighbor, but the neighbor was not home. Apparently, the car which Rav Pam had ordered had already come and the neighbor had mistakenly taken it. Rav Pam, therefore, returned to the car and asked the driver to take him to the wedding.

However, he then became concerned: what if the neighbor had in fact found some other means of transportation and the car which he had summoned had not really arrived? If this had happened, then he had caused the driver and the service to lose

Surrounded by "family" at the wedding of his son R' Asher. Standing (left to right): Rav Pam, Rabbi Moshe Wolfson, Rabbi Yitzchak Yaakov Sekulah, Rabbi Zeidel Epstein; seated: Rabbi Nesanel Quinn, Rabbi Yaakov Kamenetsky, the chasan

money. Though the loss would have been caused indirectly, according to Rabbi Akiva Eiger, he would be liable to pay.

It was this thought which had upset him so much that his blood pressure had risen.

His "Tzava'ah"

On a number of occasions over the years, Rav Pam delivered public addresses on the subject of honesty in business. Perhaps the most memorable address of all was not delivered in person. Rav Pam was to have addressed the national convention of Agudath Israel in November 2000, but poor health made this impossible. Instead, his address was videotaped in his home and then shown at the convention's Thursday night session. Rabbi Elya Svei later referred to this address as Rav Pam's *tzava'ah* (ethical will) to the generation. In that address, Rav Pam said:

"The Gemara teaches us that when a person stands before the Heavenly Court for judgment after departing this world, he is asked six questions concerning his behavior during his lifetime. The first question is, "Did you conduct your

With Rabbi Elya Svei

business dealings *b'emunah*, with faith?" — that is, with honesty. The word *emunah* can also mean, *with faith in Hashem*. Did your dealings reflect the belief that one's earnings are decreed from Heaven and that one cannot gain anything that Hashem has not granted him?

"... A Jew is bound by the same rules of conduct no matter whom he deals with," said Rav Pam. He then quoted the teachings of Rambam:

> *Should one act dishonestly [with any human being], the Torah refers to him as "disgusting."*
>
> *... The Gemara states that it is absolutely forbidden to mislead anyone, including non-Jews, all the more so when it can lead to chillul Hashem ... [In addition], such conduct has a negative impact on one's own midos, and even worse, such behavior and the people who engage in it are despicable in the eyes of Hashem.*

Rav Pam continued:

> *... A road that can ultimately lead to chillul Hashem can never yield worthwhile results ... Every Jew, especially one who is seen as representing the Torah, must be ready to give his life for Kiddush Hashem. And he must be prepared to show his love of Hashem with all that he owns. Certainly there is never an excuse for actions that might possibly — no matter how slight the chance — lead to chillul Hashem, whatever the goal.*

The Chofetz Chaim's Warning

Rav Pam related the following story:

In Radin, there lived a Jew who davened regularly in the Chofetz Chaim's yeshivah. He prayed at a *shtender* (lectern) that he owned.

One day, the man entered the beis midrash for Shacharis and discovered that his *shtender* had been moved from its place, probably by a *bachur* who had moved it for use in the place where he was studying. The man walked through the beis midrash searching for the *shtender* but could not find it.

The Chofetz Chaim, from his seat at the eastern wall, had watched as the man searched. Afterwards, throughout the davening, the Chofetz Chaim was not his usual, composed self; it was obvious that something was troubling him. After *chazaras hashatz*, the Chofetz Chaim tapped on the *bimah* for silence and said, "Reb ________ is missing his *shtender*; apparently, someone borrowed it without permission and did not return it.

"I do not want to be told who took it! But I wish to say this: The *bachur* who took the *shtender* may one day serve as a rav of a community, and there is something that he must know. Often, when a rav officiates at a wedding and is in need of two valid *eidim* (witnesses), he himself serves as one of the *eidim*. But the *bachur* should realize

The Chofetz Chaim towards the end of his life

that in his case, he must seek *two* witnesses, for he himself would not qualify as a kosher witness (for he has been guilty of theft)!"

Advice to His Talmidim

As mentioned above, the *bachurim* of Torah Vodaath organize an annual Purim fund-raising drive for Keren Yitzchak Zvi, which provides funding for Chinuch Atzmai schools. In 1993, the yeshivah rented 80 costumes for talmidim to wear as they went from house to house on Purim. After Purim, the campaign's director realized that the rental company had mistakenly billed him for only 74 costumes; as a result, the bill was $180 less than it should have been. Someone thought that since the error would result in a gain for *tzedakah*, it would be proper not to report it. When asked, Rav Pam immediately said to return the money. A call was made to the store owner, who said that he

At Rav Pam's table on Purim

had already noticed the error and he was grateful and impressed that the yeshivah had, on its own, returned the money.

A talmid who was studying to be an accountant asked Rav Pam the following: He was required to submit a report for a certain course and a friend of his in the same class had come up with an idea. Four or five friends would divide the research needed for the report and then share their knowledge with each other. "This way," said the talmid, "I'll have much more time to learn [Torah]." He wanted to know if the plan was proper.

Rav Pam replied: Accounting is a field in which there is much room for dishonesty. A few numbers changed or omitted can make a world of difference. "How will you do your work honestly as an accountant," Rav Pam asked the young man, "if your education to prepare you for that work is being done dishonestly?"

Once, a member of the Torah Vodaath kollel received a large sum of money as a gift from his grandparents, to be used towards the purchase of a home. When he and his wife "went to contract" on their new home, the young man wrote out a check for $30,000 as the down payment. The young man was surprised when his next bank statement showed that the money had not been deducted from his account. After the next month's statement arrived and still showed the money in the account, it became clear that a major mistake had occurred; the bank had transferred the $30,000 to the house's seller but had not deducted the money from the buyer's account. In all probability, the money would never be deducted — unless the young man would inform the bank manager of the error.

The young man and his wife had been living on a very tight budget and therefore, he had planned to leave kollel at year's end and enter the business world. However, with an unexpected $30,000 in the bank, he would be able to remain in kollel for at least another year.

He brought the matter before Rav Pam. Rav Pam responded without hesitation, "That is not the way to remain in kollel; return the money." Later, Rav Pam was happy to learn that Rabbi Shlomo Zalman Auerbach had ruled the same way in a similar case.

Three Conditions

The son of one of Rav Pam's former talmidim was about to begin his first job, in a Manhattan office where the boss was a non-religious Jew and the workers were gentiles. The father told his son that before he began working, he should meet with Rav Pam and present any questions he might have relating to his job.

The young man had one question for Rav Pam: Given that he was going to be the only Orthodox Jew in the office, should he perhaps not wear a yarmulka at work?

Rav Pam said that this was out of the question; if taking off his yarmulka was the only way he could work there, he should not take the job. However, said Rav Pam, "To succeed there, make sure to fulfill these three conditions: you must be the hardest worker in the office, the most honest worker in the office, and the most pleasant worker in the office."

Many years ago, Rav Pam told his class the famous statement of the Vilna Gaon that every Jew is hinted to somewhere in the Torah. Furthermore, the Gaon said that he himself was hinted to in the words אֶבֶן שְׁלֵמָה וָצֶדֶק יִהְיֶה לָּךְ, *A perfect and honest weight shall you have* (*Devarim* 25:15), for the words אֶבֶן שְׁלֵמָה stand for אֵלִיָּהוּ בֶּן שְׁלֹמֹה.

Hearing this, a talmid in the class whispered to the boy next to him, "And Rebbi is alluded to in the very next words of that *pasuk*: אֵיפָה שְׁלֵמָה וָצֶדֶק יִהְיֶה לָּךְ, *a perfect and honest measure you shall have*, for the letters of the word אֵיפָה, when rearranged, stand for אַבְרָהָם יַעֲקֹב הַכֹּהֵן פַּאם."

Rav Pam smiled upon overhearing the comment.

It certainly seems fitting that the man who in our generation symbolized *midos* perfection and honesty should be hinted to in a *pasuk* which speaks of *a perfect and honest measure*.

CHAPTER TWELVE

So Great, So Humble

Anavah, humility, says the *Ramban*, is the most important *midah* of all. Through humility, a person will grow in his *yiras Shamayim*. The Steipler Gaon writes that when a person is truly humble, he can attain a very great level of *emunah* (faith) in Hashem.

Being humble does not mean thinking, "I am a nobody." A person cannot accomplish very much if he lacks self-esteem. It is important to recognize one's abilities and accomplishments. Being humble means to understand that without Hashem's constant help, no one can accomplish anything. It also means to recognize that whatever we have accomplished might be only a fraction of our potential. Therefore, even after we have accomplished a lot, we should not become arrogant and boastful. Perhaps Hashem expects much more from us, and will in fact hold us accountable for not accomplishing more.

A Torah leader is by definition a humble person. Rav Pam's humility, however, was incredible.

Like Everyone Else

Once, a neighbor of Rebbetzin Pam heard that she was not feeling well and called to inquire about her. Rav Pam answered the phone, informed the woman that his wife was resting and suggested that she try calling back later. After an hour or two had passed, the woman's phone rang. "Hello," the caller said, "this is Avraham Pam. Would you like to speak to my wife now?"

In his last years, Rav Pam often made phone calls to raise funds for Shuvu and other worthy causes. Once, he phoned the office of a wealthy Jew in Toronto. When the secretary asked who was calling, he replied, "My name is Avraham Pam. Mr. _______ probably does not know me, but you can tell him that I am the father of Rabbi Dovid Pam [who is a rav in Toronto]." The wealthy man later expressed his amazement that Rav Pam assumed that people outside the New York area had not heard of him!

On Erev Rosh Hashanah, when close talmidim would call or visit to wish him a good year, Rav Pam would sometimes say, "Thank you for being my friend." At Shuvu gatherings,

With his mechutan, Rabbi Berel Belsky

With his friend Rabbi Yaakov Pasternak, Rav of Ahavas Achim in Kensington

he would refer to his talmidim R' Avraham Biderman and R' Gedaliah Weinberger as "my friends."

One night, a talmid at Torah Vodaath was leaving the beis midrash when he noticed a friend who studied at another yeshivah, whose first name was Avraham, leaving the building. "Good night, Avraham," the talmid called. Rav Pam, who was leaving the building after delivering his weekly *shiur* to almuni, thought that he was being addressed. He turned around and said, "Good night."

The next day, the talmid apologized profusely to Rav Pam. He explained that he had called to someone else and that he would never have had the audacity to refer to Rav Pam by his first name. Rav Pam assured him that he had done nothing wrong, and seeing that he felt bad, Rav Pam invited the talmid to join him and his rebbetzin that Friday night for the Shabbos meal.

A Seat Near the Bimah

The Gemara states that leaders of the community, the rabbanim and roshei yeshivah, should sit at the head of the congregation, by the *Mizrach* (Eastern) wall of the beis midrash. Rav Pam was an exception to this rule. When he moved to the Kensington neighborhood in the 1970s, a few blocks from Torah Vodaath, Rabbi Gedaliah Schorr invited him to sit at the Eastern wall. Rav Pam, however, chose a seat in the center of the beis midrash near the *bimah*. During learning sessions as well, when he was available for talmidim to discuss their learning, Rav Pam sat on the side of the beis midrash in

At his davening seat in the center of the beis midrash.

the center of the aisle. It seems that due to his unusual level of humility he felt he could not sit in the front with the other roshei yeshivah.

Even after Rav Schorr's passing, when Rav Pam was recognized as Rosh HaYeshivah of Torah Vodaath, he did not change his seat.

On visits to the family of his son R' Dovid in Toronto, Rav Pam often davened at Kollel Avreichim. Though the Rosh Kollel, Rabbi Shlomo Miller, invited him to sit at the Eastern wall, Rav Pam always insisted on taking a regular seat some two or three rows from the front of the beis midrash. Once, Rabbi Miller asked Rav Pam why he would not sit up front. He replied, "איך האב מורא פון כבוד *(I am afraid of [receiving] honor).*"

Only on Rosh Hashanah and Yom Kippur did Rav Pam agree to sit at the Eastern wall during davening. At first, he did this because he wanted to assist the elderly Rav Chinitz, who had been a *maggid shiur* at Torah Vodaath decades ago. When Rav Chinitz' health forced him to remain at home for the *Yamim*

Rav Pam, at his learning seat on the side of the beis midrash, with Rabbi Leibel Wulliger

Nora'im, Rav Pam's talmidim told him that his regular seat had been sold for the days of Yom Tov, and returning to it for Rosh Hashanah and Yom Kippur would be inconveniencing someone else.

When Rosh Hashanah fell on Thursday and Friday, Rav Pam returned to his regular seat on Friday night before *Maariv*. It was with obvious delight that he told his son, R' Asher, "Now I can go back to my regular seat!"

"Have Pity"

When R' Asher Pam's first son was born, it was Rav Pam who insisted that his son's Rosh Yeshivah, Rabbi Shneur Kotler, serve as *sandak*. When R' Asher told this to R' Shneur, he replied that Rav Pam should be given the honor. At the bris, R' Shneur told Rav Pam, "The *zeide* (grandfather)

With the present Lakewood Rosh Yeshivah, Rabbi Aryeh Malkiel Kotler

With Reb Yaakov outside the main building of Camp Ohr Shraga

should be *sandak*." Rav Pam replied with wonderment, "The Lakewood Rosh Yeshivah should not be *sandak*?" When Reb Shneur repeated his argument, tears welled up in Rav Pam's eyes and he pleaded: "האט רחמנות אויפ'ן קינד און זייט סנדק, *Have pity on the child and be sandak*." R' Shneur, taken aback, accepted the honor without another word.

A visitor lamented to Rav Pam: "I just returned from Eretz Yisrael and I regret having wasted Rav Shach's time! I went to see him and sat with him for 20 minutes. After I left, I asked myself, 'What did I just do? Rav Shach did not need this visit!

Because I wanted the *zechus* of sitting with him, did I have a right to take up 20 minutes of his life?' "

After the man left, Rav Pam said to his son, R' Asher, "This is the reason why I have not visited R' Yaakov [Kamenetsky] all the years that he has lived in Monsey. Why would I go? Because *I* want to visit with R' Yaakov. But what will R' Yaakov have from my visit? Do I have a right to take up his valuable time because I want to spend time with him?"

Rav Pam was unaware of a comment R' Yaakov had once made. "If I did not think that he would find it uncomfortable, I would attend Rav Pam's Erev Shabbos shmuessen. His pure words would have a great effect on me."

Hard Like Iron

The Gemara teaches, "Any talmid chacham who is not as hard as iron, is not a talmid chacham" (*Taanis* 4a). While humility is a great and crucial *midah*, a talmid chacham needs to be firm when the situation calls for it.

Once, an organization's leader was being challenged by some members of the board who were unhappy with how he was running the organization. A meeting was called to settle the matter. At the meeting, sharp criticism of this individual was voiced and it appeared that those who were challenging him would succeed in weakening his power and changing the organization's direction.

Rav Pam knew this individual better than anyone else; he was convinced that the man's actions were without fault and that attempts to tamper with his work would only hamper the organization's activities. To everyone's shock, Rav Pam took the floor and declared that if the only way the organization could continue was if the proposed major changes were implemented, then he would rather see the organization close down.

The meeting ended with no changes being adopted; to this day, the organization is very successful and respected.

Offering Rebuke

When we see another Jew sin, we are obligated to rebuke him in a respectful way (*Vayikra* 19:17). Despite his deep humility, Rav Pam would offer rebuke when necessary.

One day, a man stopped him in the street to voice some derogatory remarks about a certain group of Orthodox Jews. Rav Pam told him, "Reb Yid, you have just said something shameful about an entire *"shevet"* (sect) in *Klal Yisrael* — and it is very difficult to do *teshuvah* for this."

Once, a meeting took place in Rav Pam's home at which were present a well-known *maggid shiur* and a businessman who was a wealthy contributor to many worthy causes. At one point, the two disagreed sharply over a certain point. The businessman became agitated and said something disrespectful to the *maggid shiur*. Rav Pam rapped on the table and said, "Such words will not be heard in my house! This man is a talmid chacham, a *marbitz Torah* (disseminator of Torah) and has guided many talmidim over the years — you must speak to him with *derech eretz*." The discussion resumed and no further outbursts occurred.

Rav Pam was able to voice his feelings in situations where others may have been afraid to do so. The above incident illustrates this. The businessman was someone from whom Rav Pam himself would request tzedakah donations. By criticizing the man, Rav Pam might have caused him to give less, or nothing at all, the next time he was asked. This possibility did not prevent Rav Pam from speaking up. If the situation called for defending the honor of Torah, nothing else mattered.

For his part, the businessman knew that Rav Pam's words flowed from a heart that was pure and kind, and that if he spoke out forcefully, he felt that this is what the Torah required him to do.

Honoring Others

Rabbi Itze'le Peterburger wrote of his master and teacher, Rabbi Yisrael Salanter: "It was amazing that while he was removed from all earthly pleasures, from physical desires and from a need for honor, nevertheless with regard to others, he understood all their needs. He was removed from the slightest desire for honor, yet he was careful to honor others."

While Rav Pam shunned any form of honor, he sought to honor others at every opportunity.

It is common for the *chasan's* family to choose who will serve as *mesader kiddushin* at his wedding. Once, a talmid informed Rav Pam of his dilemma. He wanted very much that his rebbi, Rav Pam, should serve as his *mesader kiddushin*, but the *kallah's* father wanted to accord this honor to Rabbi Simcha Bunim Ehrenfeld, the Mattesdorfer Rav, to whom he was very close.

Rav Pam replied: "The Mattesdorfer Rav is an *ehrlicher Yid* and your father-in-law's wishes should be respected. I will come as a friend."

When he was not the only elderly talmid chacham scheduled to speak at a *simchah*, he would often ask the *baal simchah* to accord the other talmid chacham the honor of speaking first.

When a talmid informed him that the bris of his son would take place on Shabbos in his home, Rav Pam (who could not attend) asked, "Will Rav ________ [who lived in the neighborhood] be attending?" "Most probably," replied the talmid. "Will he be given a *kibud* (honor)?" Rav Pam asked. When the talmid replied that he had not planned on this, Rav Pam told him that this talmid chacham must be accorded an honor.

> *Once, a talmid asked whether Rav Pam could attend the bris of his son. It was to be held on a Sunday morning, at the same time that a Torah Vodaath board of directors meeting was scheduled, one which Rav Pam was to attend. Rav Pam changed the time of the board meeting so that he could attend the bris. It was only when he arrived at the bris that the baal simchah asked him to serve as sandak. "Perhaps there is someone else whom you would like to honor," Rav Pam replied. "I'm happy just to be here."*

Being greeted by the Mattersdorfer Rav.
Rabbi Aharon Schechter is in the background.

In 1999, the Gerrer Rosh Yeshivah, Rabbi Shaul Alter, visited America and made an appointment to call on Rav Pam at his office in Mesivta Torah Vodaath. When the phone rang with the message that Rabbi Alter would soon be arriving, Rav Pam was in his office learning with a talmid. "I need an *eitzah* (advice)," he said to his talmid. "The Gerrer Rosh Yeshivah will soon be arriving. It would not be right for me to sit on this side of the desk in my armchair and have the Gerrer Rosh Yeshivah on the opposite side in a plain chair. What should I do?"

Reciting the berachos at a bris

The talmid was astounded by the question. The Gerrer Rosh Yeshivah, a renowned talmid chacham, was decades younger than Rav Pam. Moreover, Rav Pam was Rosh HaYeshivah of Torah Vodaath and it was certainly appropriate for him to sit in his armchair in *his* office at *his* yeshivah.

When the talmid suggested that the desk be moved in such a way that two armchairs could be placed on the same side of it, Rav Pam said, "I cannot move around the furniture. I am only a one-third partner in this office," which was shared by Rav Pam, Rabbi Moshe Wolfson and Rabbi Yosef Savitsky.

In his office at Mesivta Torah Vodaath following Shacharis

Moments later, there was a knock on the door; the Gerrer Rosh Yeshivah had arrived. Rav Pam greeted his distinguished guest and then placed two regular chairs side by side, so that he and his guest could sit next to each other as they conversed.

Once, Rav Wolfson was sitting in that office speaking with a talmid when there was a knock at the door. Many have the habit of knocking on a door and then opening it slightly, but this time it did not open at all. "Whoever is knocking is a *baal*

With Rabbi Moshe Wolfson

derech eretz," Rav Wolfson remarked before saying, "Come in." The door opened and in walked Rav Pam.

A ride was arranged to take Rav Pam home from a *simchah*. When the driver, a yeshivah bachur, attempted to pick up Rav Pam's bag to carry it to the car, Rav Pam stopped him. "Please let me carry it myself," he said. "If you carry it for me, then you are acting like my 'driver.' You are not my 'driver.' You are my friend."

Honored and Pained

As a person who sought to honor others at every opportunity, Rav Pam was deeply pained by the

With Rabbi Aharon Schechter

thought that he might have deprived someone of an honor, even indirectly.

An American yeshivah student had devoted his summer vacations and other free time to help bring Russian immigrant children to the path of Torah. He frequently consulted *gedolei Torah* concerning his work and they had deep respect and admiration for him and his accomplishments.

When the young man's wedding date was set, he invited both Rav Pam and the Rosh Yeshivah of Mesivta Rabbeinu Chaim Berlin, Rabbi Aharon Schechter, to the wedding. Both responded that, unfortunately, there was another wedding that night which they both had to attend. For Rav Pam it was a family wedding, and for Rav Schechter it was a *simchah* of a member of the Chaim Berlin *hanhalah*.

At that wedding, someone approached both roshei yeshivah and offered to take them to the young man's chuppah ceremony, which was scheduled to begin one half-hour after the first chuppah. They accepted the offer and as soon as the first chuppah ended, they were driven to the

Left to right: Rabbi Aharon Schechter, Rabbi Shmuel Kamenetsky, Rav Pam

other wedding. They arrived there as the *chasan* (groom) was about to walk down the aisle. Upon seeing the two roshei yeshivah, the *chasan* became so overcome with emotion that he had to return to the chasan's room for a few moments before being led to the chuppah. Rav Pam was called upon to read the *kesubah* and Rav Schechter was honored with reciting the last of the *sheva berachos*. Immediately after the chuppah, the two roshei yeshivah were driven back to the other wedding.

As the driver later expressed it, "This was a true fulfillment of the mitzvah to bring joy to a *chasan* and *kallah*." Rav Pam's feeling, however, was one of distress. "Why did they have to give me a *kibud* (honor)?" he lamented. "I didn't come for a *kibud* — I came to be *mechabed* (accord honor to) the *chasan*! If I was given a *kibud*, that means that someone else did not receive a *kibud* which had been intended for him!"

In his later years, Rav Pam would sometimes tell his family how much it bothered him when he was introduced as "*Hagaon* (the Torah genius)," for he felt unworthy of this title. Yet, he was very upset when other roshei yeshivah were not introduced with this title.

It happened at his grandchild's wedding. At the chuppah ceremony, one of Rav Pam's grandsons was announcing the *kibudim*. When he called up a rosh yeshivah as "Harav ... " Rav Pam was obviously distressed. "You have to say *'Hagaon'* when such a person is called up," he said.

When the rosh yeshivah stepped up onto the platform, Rav Pam apologized to him. "He is a young *bachur*," he explained, referring to his grandson. "He was unaware of the proper introduction for the Rosh Yeshivah." Before the next rosh yeshivah was called up, Rav Pam instructed his grandson, "Say '*Hagaon* Harav,' rather than 'Harav *Hagaon*' — it is more *bechavod'ig* (honorable)."

Rav Pam's concern for someone else's honor remained with him to the very end. The last wedding he attended was that of his granddaughter Nechama Pam to Yitzchak Schwarzman. It took place in June, some two months before

Rav Pam as mesader kiddushin at a grandchild's wedding

Rav Pam's passing, when he was already quite ill. It brought great joy to the family when, the night before the wedding, it was decided that Rav Pam would be well enough to attend and, as the kallah's grandfather, would serve as *mesader kiddushin*.

However, on that same night Rav Pam told his son R' Aharon, the kallah's father, "I cannot be *mesader kiddushin.* That honor belongs to the *chasan's* family to bestow, and his family is very close to [the Mirrer Rosh Yeshivah] Rav Shmuel Berenbaum. *He* should be *mesader kiddushin.*"

R' Aharon Pam was certain that the *chasan's* family would want Rav Pam, as grandfather, to officiate, but out of respect for his father, he contacted his *mechutan*, Rabbi Aharon

Rav Pam, at his seat near the bimah, and Rabbi Shmuel Berenbaum during krias HaTorah at Mesivtah Torah Vodaath.

Schwarzman, to discuss the matter. Rabbi Schwarzman was quick to respond that, without a doubt, Rav Berenbaum would never accept the honor knowing that the *kallah* was Rav Pam's granddaughter. However, to satisfy Rav Pam, he spoke to Rav Berenbaum, who firmly declined the honor.

The following night, Rav Pam was brought to the chuppah in a wheelchair; he officiated and stood throughout the chuppah ceremony. Rav Berenbaum was honored with reading the *kesubah*. After the *kesubah* had been read and Rav Berenbaum had returned to his seat, Rav Pam turned to his son and said, "Please go to Rav Shmuel now and ask him how long the *eidim* (two witnesses) should remain outside the *yichud* room after the chuppah." R' Aharon was quite surprised by the request. His father had officiated at countless chuppos and surely was able on his own to instruct the *eidim* regarding their responsibilities. Apparently this was Rav Pam's way of honoring Rav Berenbaum, as if Rav Pam was merely representing him as *mesader kiddushin*.

Before the ceremony continued, R' Aharon stepped off the chuppah platform, made his way to Rav Berenbaum and asked him the question. At first Rav Berenbaum refused to answer, out of respect for Rav Pam, but upon being convinced that this was Rav Pam's desire, he offered his opinion.

More than Meets the Eye

Rav Pam did more than see the good in others. He recognized that within every Jew lies the potential for greatness. As the Mishnah states, "Do not be scornful of any person ... for you have no person without his hour" (*Avos* 4:3). It is not difficult to honor others when one truly believes that they are deserving of honor.

In Rav Pam's words:

> *We tend to underestimate people while they are alive. There are people who do marvelous things that no one knows about. I personally knew simple people, people about whom no one would think anything special, who did beautiful deeds that would befit gedolim.*
>
> *There was a simple woman, a widow, who would do housekeeping for my mother. She did this sort of work in the homes of a number of rabbanim. She could not have earned very much. This woman had a friend, also a widow, who was in need of a loan. The housekeeper lent her friend $100, quite a sum of money 50 years ago. Shortly thereafter the borrower died without having repaid the loan.*
>
> *My mother happened to be walking near this housekeeper at the funeral procession for that woman. The housekeeper was whispering, "Ich bin dir mochel, ich bin dir mochel (I forgive you, I forgive you)." She knew that her money was lost and she did not want her friend to be held accountable for this in Heaven.*
>
> *Did anyone know how much beauty and fineness was hidden in this housekeeper's neshamah? There are others like her, people who do mighty deeds with such simplicity, without thinking that they are doing something great, and no one knows about it.*

Rav Pam would relate another incident as an example of the hidden greatness of simple Jews:

Many years ago, Rav Pam delivered a weekly *Tanach shiur* in an East New York shul. Once, a storm raged and Rav Pam debated whether or not to venture outside. He decided that while few people would be going outside that night, he was obligated to go to the shul on the chance that someone might come for his *shiur*. Three or four people attended the *shiur* that night. One of them was a man who was totally unlearned and never attended any *shiurim* because he did not understand anything. When someone asked him why he had come that night, he replied, "I thought that few people, or perhaps no one else, would come. *Someone* had to be here for the *shiur*!"

Honoring Gedolim

Rav Pam displayed great reverence towards other *gedolim*. This was a reflection of his genuine regard for them and his humble view of himself.

He enjoyed a warm relationship with the previous Rosh Yeshivah of Mesivta Torah Vodaath, Rabbi Gedaliah Schorr, who — like Rav Pam — started out as a talmid in the yeshivah. Rav Pam once remarked that he was amazed by Rav Schorr's encyclopedic knowledge of Midrash and on occasion would ask him for the source of a particular midrash.

When Rav Pam's son R' Asher was a boy of 12, he owned a collection of photos of *gedolei Yisrael* of the past century, most of whom had been leaders in pre-Holocaust Europe. One day, a friend of Rav Pam who had learned in the great yeshivos of pre-war Europe was looking through the album. He did not recognize the face of the last *gadol* in the album, who appeared considerably younger than all the previous ones. "That is the Rosh Yeshivah of Torah

With Rabbi Gedaliah Schorr at the bar mitzvah of Rav Schorr's grandson. Rav Schorr's mechutan, Rabbi Moshe Shimshon Lesser, is in the foreground.

Vodaath, Rav Gedaliah Schorr," Asher told the man. The man, who was about Rav Schorr's age, exclaimed to Rav Pam, "R' Avraham, you hear this? Your son has a picture of Rav Gedaliah Schorr in his *gedolim* album. Soon they are going to put *your* picture in *gedolim* albums!" Rav Pam laughed heartily and responded that Rav Schorr *deserved* to be in such a photo collection ...

When the Pams lived in East Flatbush, an annual Melaveh Malkah was held at a local shul to benefit Mesivtha Tifereth Jerusalem. The Melaveh Malkah was always graced by the presence of the yeshivah's revered Rosh Yeshivah, Rabbi Moshe Feinstein.

One year, on the night of the Melaveh Malkah, Rav Pam realized that circumstances would force him to arrive late to the gathering. However, he instructed his son Asher, "The melavah malkah is called for 9:00. Be there at 8:45."

With Rabbi Moshe Feinstein at a wedding.

Asher respectfully replied that such gatherings never begin punctually; if he arrived at 9:15, he would probably still be "on time." His father responded, "R' Moshe may arrive on time and it will be a *bizayon* (disgrace) if no one is there to greet him."

Asher arrived there at 8:58. Punctually at 9:00, R' Moshe arrived. The only ones who were there to greet him were the shul's Rav and Asher Pam.

He would praise the public addresses of the late Telshe Rosh Yeshivah, Rabbi Mordechai Gifter. In the years before he spent Shabbos at the Agudath Israel annual convention, Rav Pam would listen to the radio broadcast of Rav Gifter's Motza'ei Shabbos convention address. He once related that he and Rav Gifter had gone for a stroll together at a Torah Umesorah convention; their talk had left a deep impression upon him. In the years when Rav Gifter was ill, Rav Pam would, from time to time, express his deep distress and would add that Rav Gifter's involvement as a leader of *Klal Yisrael* was sorely missed.

At one Torah Umesorah convention, Rav Gifter, in his major address, related a thought in the name of "*der golde'ne Rav Pam*" (the golden Rav Pam) and he would refer to Rav Pam this way in private as well.

Rabbi Mordechai Gifter

At one point during Rav Gifter's illness, when he had hardly spoken for days, a visitor entered his room and introduced himself as a grandson of Rav Pam. Rav Gifter's eyes shone and he said, "You have a precious *zeide*!"

For many years, Rav Pam and Rabbi Avigdor HaKohen Miller lived in the same neighborhood, first in East New York and later in East Flatbush. They, too, held one another in great esteem.

When Rabbi Miller moved to East New York, Rabbi Yitzchak Hutner told him, "Keep your eye on R' Avraham Pam — he is a special young man."

When paying a *shivah* visit to Rav Miller's family, Rav Pam said that while Rav Miller was officially a rav, he was actually a rosh yeshivah, for he succeeded in creating a *kehillah* of bnei Torah whose lives revolve around Torah study.

When a class from the Lakewood Cheder School visited Rav Pam, he asked where they were heading next. When told that Rav Miller's home was their next destination, Rav Pam said, "You should know that Rav Miller is from the *ziknei kehunah* (senior *kohanim*) and from the *tzaddikei hador* (righteous of the generation)."

In one of his famous Thursday night lectures, Rav Miller said: "There is a Jew, a tzaddik, who lives on East 7th Street, and his name is Rav Pam. Rav [Yitzchak] Hutner told me many years ago, 'This man is an *adam gadol*' (great Torah personality)."

Rabbi Avigdor Miller

Another time, Rav Miller told his listeners, "The day will come when you will say, 'Ah! Rav Pam! Where is Rav Pam?' "

Public Gatherings

After the passing of the Steipler Gaon, Rabbi Yaakov Yisrael Kanievsky, a well-attended memorial gathering was held in Brooklyn. The program included many addresses by leading roshei yeshivah, Rav Pam among them. Late in the program as the next speaker made his way to the podium, Rav Pam stood up from his seat at the dais and announced, "Please excuse me, but a chuppah is soon to take place and the people are waiting

The Steipler Gaon

for me." In this way, he made it clear that had it been possible, he would have remained for the speeches that would follow.

In his last years, when illness made it painful for him to sit for long periods of time, he was asked to attend a gathering marking the launching of a new *kiruv* (outreach) organization. He debated whether or not to attend. Finally, he decided to go and to stay for a short while.

But he remained for the entire program, which lasted some two hours. He later told his family, "There were rabbanim there; how could I walk out?"

With Rabbi Yaakov Weinberg

With Rabbi Tuvia Goldstein

With the Bobover Rav (Rabbi Shlomo Halberstam)

With Rabbi Chaim Pinchus Scheinberg. To the left is Rabbi Simchah Scheinberg.

With Rabbi Zelik Epstein

With the Rachmistrivka Rebbe. Rabbi Aharon Braun is in the background.

With the Skverer Rebbe

With his cousin Rabbi Noach Feldman

With Rabbi Yitzchak Feigelstock

With Rabbi Shmuel Feivelson

Left to right: Rav Pam, Rabbi David Feinstein, Rabbi Reuven Feinstein

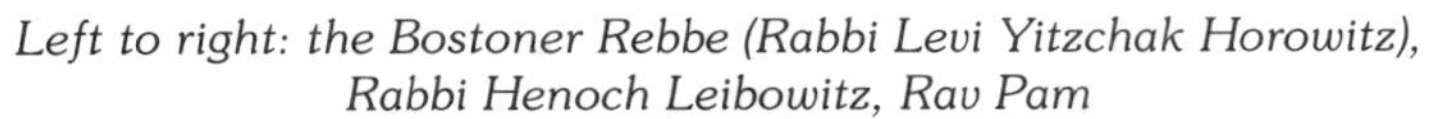

Left to right: the Bostoner Rebbe (Rabbi Levi Yitzchak Horowitz), Rabbi Henoch Leibowitz, Rav Pam

Holy and Pure

About ten years ago, a well-known family was observing *shivah*. One of the mourners was non-religious. One afternoon, Rav Pam came to pay a *shivah* call. This mourner was startled. "Who is that? He is a holy man!" he said in a whisper.

He was right, but how did he know? How could one tell that a small man in an ordinary suit was holy?

Those close to Rav Pam were not surprised. The holiness of his *neshamah* shone through, unmistakably.

Rabbi Elya Svei once said of Rav Pam: "Everyone knows that from the Rosh Yeshivah there shone a light, a G-dly light, a light which called forth: 'See what can be attained through Torah.' "

Beneath Rav Pam's simple, down-to-earth style lay a greatness which, at times, seemed to endow him with *Ruach HaKodesh* (Divine Inspiration).

Someone close to Rav Pam was presented with an opportunity for an important venture which would require a large sum of money which he did not have. Rav Pam told him that the venture was a worthy one and he should pursue it. "But from where will I get the money?" the person asked. "Good friends will come forward to help you," Rav Pam said.

As the man walked home from Rav Pam's funeral, he was approached by a well-to-do acquaintance. The man had heard about his plans. "You probably need money," he offered. The man then withdrew his checkbook and wrote out a check for a large sum.

A bachur, whose family was close to Rav Pam, was learning well but was troubled by the thought that perhaps he could learn even better in another yeshivah. The next time he and his father visited Rav Pam, the father mentioned, as he had done in the past, which yeshivah his son attended. However, this time Rav Pam responded as never before. "Yeshivah ___________? It is a yeshivah *mesugal* for *aliyah* (ideal for spiritual growth)!" When they left the house, the bachur told his father, "Rav Pam has answered my question."

Once, a man who had recovered from a serious illness was plagued by fears that he would have a relapse. When he expressed his fears to Rav Pam, the tzaddik replied cryptically, "Why are you worried? Don't you realize that the doctor who treated you was born in order to save your life?"

Some time later, this man called that doctor's office to make an appointment for someone else. The secretary said, "Mr. __________, do you mean you don't know? The doctor passed away soon after he finished treating you."

At the wedding of his grandson, Binyamin Pam

In the last decade of his life, Rav Pam had a daily learning session with his grandson, R' Binyamin. As a rule, Rav Pam would not answer the phone during these sessions. On rare occasions, Rav Pam would tell his grandson, "Answer the phone; maybe it's important." His grandson relates that in every such instance, the call was very important: a Rosh Yeshivah calling from Eretz Yisrael, an emergency situation that had suddenly come up, etc.

With Rav Nesanel Quinn

In an address on the first *yahrtzeit* of Rav Pam, his lifelong friend and colleague, Rabbi Nesanel Quinn, said: "Praiseworthy are you, Rav Avraham Pam. בָּרוּךְ אַתָּה בְּבוֹאֶךָ, Blessed are you, who descended to this world as a pure *neshamah*. וּבָרוּךְ אַתָּה בְּצֵאתֶךָ, and blessed are you, who departed this world the same pure *neshamah*."

CHAPTER THIRTEEN

Love of Mitzvos

Big and Small

Our Sages teach: "Be as careful in performing a 'minor' mitzvah as in a 'major' mitzvah, for you do not know the reward for mitzvos" (*Avos* 2:1). "For you do not know the reward" can be explained as "for you cannot imagine the incredible reward" for even the most seemingly "minor" mitzvah.

In his *avodas Hashem* (service of G-d), Rav Pam showed a true love of Hashem and His mitzvos. He was careful in

following every detail of halachah, even in what might be considered "minor mitzvos."

All his life, Rav Pam stood during *krias haTorah* (the Torah reading). In his last years, when his posture was bent and standing was difficult, he asked three men to form a *beis din* and be *matir neder* (annul a vow) so that he could sit when the Torah was read. Yet even after that, he almost always stood. When someone asked him why he continued to stand when he was certainly permitted to sit, he replied with a smile, "Now that I was *matir neder*, there is no longer a *yetzer hara* to sit!"

All in the Mind

One evening as Rav Pam left a wedding hall, he said to the musician, "Thank you for your wonderful music." The musician smiled and replied, "Well, that's my job!" Rav Pam

Thanking the musicians at the conclusion of his son's wedding

responded, "I'll tell you what to do. From now on, when you play your music, have in mind that you want to fulfill the mitzvah of bringing joy to the *chasan* and *kallah*, to their families and friends." The musician did not understand how his work could be considered a mitzvah. "But I'm getting paid to do it!" he argued. "It doesn't matter," said Rav Pam, "it still can be a mitzvah."

Once, Rav Pam told his dentist: "I envy you. You do *chesed* all day. People come to you in pain and you make them feel better."

The dentist replied, "It's a fringe benefit of the profession." He meant to say that while he was a dentist to earn a living, the result of dental work is that the patient feels better.

"You're wrong," said Rav Pam. "Your profession is to do *chesed* with people. A fringe benefit of it is that you earn a living."

When visiting Minsk, the legendary tzaddik Rabbi Elya Dushnitzer met a pharmacist who was a great *yarei Shamayim*; he was the head of the *chevrah kaddisha* (burial society), the *hachnasas kallah* (poor brides) fund, and other worthy causes. R' Elya asked the man how he had come to be at the forefront of so many mitzvah activities. The man replied:

> *Many years ago, I had strayed far from the path of Torah. One day, I met the Chofetz Chaim and he asked me what I did for a living. When I told him that I was a pharmacist, he said to me in his sincere way:*
>
> *"When you prepare your medicines and bring them to the sick, have in mind that you are fulfilling the mitzvah of bikur cholim and helping to heal a fellow Jew. That way, you will be transforming an act which is merely a way to earn money into a precious mitzvah."*
>
> *The Chofetz Chaim's words, spoken so earnestly and with such purity, made a deep impression upon me. It was after that encounter that I returned to a life of Torah, and I have tried ever since to fulfill the Chofetz Chaim's advice.*

Tefillah

At the conclusion of his weekly *shiur* to alumni, Rav Pam would daven Maariv together with his talmidim. One week, he davened Maariv before the *shiur* because he was to be driven somewhere when the *shiur* ended. As he and his driver walked down the hallway at the *shiur's* end, they heard the *minyan* beginning the *berachah* of *Ahavas Olam*. Rav Pam stopped and told his companion, "I would like to say [the first *pasuk* of] *Shema* with the *tzibur* (congregation)."

Leading Bircas HaMazon

One weekday at Mesivta Torah Vodaath, a talmid noticed Rav Pam reciting *Ein Keilokeinu* at the conclusion of Shacharis, along with the minyan which prays in *Nusach Sefard*. Aware that Rav Pam davened from the *Nusach Ashkenaz* text, which includes this prayer only on Shabbos, the talmid asked him about this. "How can I not say such a beautiful *tefillah*?" was his simple reply.

During the chazzan's repetition of *Shemoneh Esrei*, Rav Pam listened carefully to every word, as the halachah states. He kept his eyes focused on the words in his siddur the entire time.

Once, a talmid spent the night of Yom Kippur in Rav Pam's home. Early the next morning, when Rav Pam washed his hands and proceeded to recite the *Asher Yatzar* blessing with great intensity, he was unaware that his talmid was listening in the next room. It took about two full minutes for him to recite this *berachah*, which many recite in mere seconds.

Rav Pam would say that Torah and tefillah go hand in hand. He would relate how the Chazon Ish would beseech Hashem for *siyata diShmaya* to discover the true meaning of the Gemara that he studied with superhuman effort. A true *ben*

Torah strives to grow in his davening just as he strives to grow in his learning.

Shabbos and Yom Tov

Some 15 years ago, Rav Pam spent a Shabbos in New York Hospital as a precaution. As he was feeling basically well, he insisted that no one stay with him over Shabbos. The family, therefore, arranged for two talmidim to visit him on Shabbos afternoon. They were surprised to find their rebbi sitting in his hospital room dressed for Shabbos. Rav Pam told them with a chuckle that on Erev Shabbos when the nurse saw him fully dressed, she suspected that he might be attempting to "escape" without being discharged. "Where are you going?" she had asked him. He explained that he had gotten dressed in honor of the Sabbath.

He once remarked that what he missed the most from the days of his childhood was the Erev Shabbos atmosphere that was common to *shtetl* life in Europe. By noontime, Shabbos preparations were complete, the men had stopped their work and many were already in their Shabbos clothing, learning or reciting *Shir HaShirim*. The women had finished their tasks in the kitchen and many were reciting *Tehillim*.

Four years before his passing, before he permitted a minyan to pray in his home on Rosh Hashanah and Yom Kippur, Rav Pam davened at home alone. Someone who had volunteered to blow shofar for Rav Pam was asked to come to his house during the break at Mesivta Torah Vodaath between Shacharis and Mussaf. During the previous night, Rav Pam had been in great pain and had not fallen asleep. In the morning, he was given pain medication, which usually causes drowsiness, and his family hoped that he would fall asleep and that the shofar would be blown for him in the late afternoon. But the knowledge that he had not yet fulfilled the mitzvah of shofar did not allow him to sleep, and therefore the *baal tokei'ah* was summoned in the morning.

In the succah of Mesivta Torah Vodaath. Rabbi Avraham Talansky is at left.

Though the man offered to ascend the stairs and sound the shofar for Rav Pam in his bedroom, Rav Pam insisted on coming downstairs, fully dressed and wrapped in his tallis.

In his succah, he would hang a poster on which he had written in Hebrew the words of *Chayei Adam*:

> *Because the kedushah of the succah is very great, it is proper to minimize plain conversation and to talk only words of kedushah and Torah in it. Certainly one should be careful to avoid speaking lashon hara or rechilus*[1] *there, or other forbidden talk.*

ולפי שקדושת סוכה גדולה מאד ראוי שלא לדבר
בה כ"א קדושה ותורה, ובכ"ש שיזהר שלא לדבר בה
לה"ר ושאר דבורים האסורים.
(חיי אדם)

Sign that Rav Pam hung in his succah

1. *Rechilus* is *lashon hara* that causes ill feelings between people.

The Joy of a Jewish Life

Rav Pam once said: "What is the definition of an '*am ha'aretz*' (ignoramus)? Someone who thinks that in order to serve Hashem, he has to give up enjoyment of life in this world in favor of life in the World to Come. A talmid chacham, however, knows the truth — that a *ben Torah* has the best of *both worlds*."

In the Torah Vodaath beis midrash during Hoshanos on Succos

Rav Pam would repeat something that the Ksav Sofer is reported to have said:

"Does a gentile really understand the pleasures of this world? Did he ever arise a few hours before dawn, drink a hot coffee and then, with a clear mind, study Torah, and immerse himself in a hot mikveh as preparation for a fiery davening?

"No, a gentile has no idea of the pleasures of this world!"

Kindling the menorah

CHAPTER FOURTEEN

A Gadol's Wisdom

hoever engages in Torah study for its own sake (lishmah) ... from him people enjoy advice and wisdom (Avos 6:1).

Rav Pam was an easy person to talk to. He had a sense of humor and made people feel at ease in his presence. Above all, he was a good listener. He would allow a person as much time as he needed to express himself, and then, slowly and deliberately, Rav Pam offered the advice which he felt was best suited for that individual and his situation.

No one will ever know how many hundreds, probably thousands, of people came to him for advice and *chizuk* (emotional strength) during his 63-year career as a rebbi and rosh yeshivah. Only Hashem knows how many hearts he healed, how many spirits he lifted.

But one thing we do know. Rav Pam had the ability to see through to the root of a problem, crystallize the issue and offer advice that one immediately felt was correct.

And he took every person's problem to heart, making it his own.

Remembering a Stranger

Rabbi Tzvi Joseph, a young talmid chacham who had never learned in Torah Vodaath and had had no personal contact with Rav Pam, related the following:

> *Several years ago, I went to see Rav Pam,* זצ"ל*, to ask if it is proper according to halachah*

for me to earn money through a certain program. Rav Pam advised me that it was not halachically correct.

Two years later on an Erev Shabbos, I received a phone call from Rav Pam. He greeted me warmly, like an old acquaintance, and said, "A short while ago, you asked a question related to דִינֵי מָמוֹנוֹת (money matters). This week someone came to me with the same question and we came up with an eitzah (solution) that I wanted to share with you."

After sharing his thoughts with me, Rav Pam then inquired about me and my family and asked how we were managing, and so on. This gadol hador took 15 minutes of his time on an Erev Shabbos to phone me, a stranger, and offer his help.

I asked Rav Pam how he remembered me two years later and he replied humbly, "Some things I forget from one day to the next and other things I remember for a while." I countered, "But how did the Rosh Yeshivah remember my name?"

He replied, "The Gemara says: ... אִי לֹא הַאי יוֹמָא כַּמָּה יוֹסֵף אִיכָּא בְּשׁוּקָא (If not for this day, there are many 'Josephs' at the market!). Nu, כַּמָּה צְבִי יוֹסֵף אִיכָּא בְּשׁוּקָא? (How many 'Tzvi Josephs' are there?) I opened the phone book, and found your name and phone number."

This kind of concern for a stranger's problem is a sign of true greatness.

Once, a bachur who had never met Rav Pam personally called to make an appointment to discuss a problem. Rav Pam told the boy a date and a time and said that they would meet at his home, not in yeshivah. The bachur was unfamiliar with the Kensington neigborhood and asked Rav Pam for directions to his home.

For some reason, the bachur had difficulty finding the house and was late for the appointment. When he finally found himself on the block where Rav Pam lived, an elderly couple was walking down the block. It was Rabbi and Rebbetzin Pam. As the hour grew late, Rav Pam surmised that the bachur could not find the house, so he and his rebbetzin went out to search for him.

Of Utmost Importance

In Rav Pam's last years when illness confined him to his home, R' Chaim Leshkowitz called for an appointment. Mr. Leshkowitz is Chairman of the Board of Torah Vodaath, and he made it clear that he needed to speak to Rav Pam

Descending the stairs outside the Torah Vodaath beis midrash.
Left to right: Rav Pam, Chaim Leshkowitz, Rabbi Boruch Diamond.

about yeshivah matters. It took three days until he was given an appointment. When he arrived that evening, a husband and wife were speaking with Rav Pam; apparently, they had come to discuss an important family issue.

After the couple left, Mr. Leshkowitz respectfully asked, "Doesn't Rebbi need to conserve his strength? It seems to me that involving oneself in such cases would be a drain on anyone. And also: Rebbi often refers to Torah Vodaath as his 'home,' the place with which he has been identified for most of his life. May I ask: Why are the yeshivah's needs not given priority?"

Rav Pam replied simply, "If I don't listen to them, they will have no one to talk to." Rav Pam considered every Jew who came to him like a member of his family; the person's needs were of the highest priority.

Urim V'Tumim

Some 25 years ago, someone approached a renowned talmid chacham to seek his advice in a personal matter. The matter was not simple and the talmid chacham did not feel qualified to offer advice. He told the person, "Ask Rav Pam; he is an *urim v'tumim*."

The *Choshen* (Breastplate) which the Kohen Gadol wore contained a slip of parchment called the *Urim V'Tumim* upon which was inscribed the Name of Hashem. It was through the power of the *Urim V'Tumim* that the letters inscribed on the stones of the *Choshen* lit up to spell answers from Heaven to important questions.

A talmid put it this way: "In the 25 years that I knew Rav Pam, I spoke with him hundreds of times. Any advice he offered that I acted upon always brought success."

Everyone's Gain

A young man whose family had been living in a rented apartment bought a three-family house. Two of the apartments were occupied at the time; one was empty. By law, the new owner could not evict the tenants who were already living there. When the young man rented out the empty apartment, he told the new tenants, a young Orthodox couple, that he was renting it to them with the understanding that he might need the apartment at any time and that they had to be prepared to move on short notice.

The day came when he needed the apartment for his family. He went to Rav Pam with the following question: His tenants were very happy in the apartment and wanted to stay there a while longer. It was becoming difficult for his own family in their present apartment, but they could manage a while longer there if necessary. Was he correct to ask the tenant to leave now, as per their agreement?

Rav Pam advised the man to act with *chesed* and allow his tenants to remain a while longer.

A few months later, one of the other tenants in the three-family house unexpectedly moved out. The other original tenant, whose apartment was adjoining the one that was now vacant, moved out shortly thereafter. The owner was now able to combine both vacant apartments into a large, comfortable apartment for his own family, while the third tenant was able to remain indefinitely. Following Rav Pam's advice to act with *chesed* led to good results for everyone.

For Every Good Cause

Whenever people came to Rav Pam with something for the benefit of Torah study or *Klal Yisrael*, he was as thrilled as if his own children had suggested it. When Rabbi Nosson Scherman and Rabbi Meir Zlotowitz spoke to him about the projected ArtScroll — later to become the Schottenstein — Talmud, he listened, probed, suggested, and gave his warm encouragement.

When Brooklyn's *Va'ad Hachnasas Orchim* (Committee for Welcoming Guests) was founded, Rav Pam was consulted regarding various details. He was delighted to hear that the organization's volunteers included Chassidim, Sephardim and products of the Lithuanian yeshivah world — a demonstration of true *achdus* (unity): "For this alone," he said, "the project is worthwhile."

Rabbi Meir Zlotowitz (right) and Rabbi Nosson Scherman (center) show Rav Pam a preview of the first draft of the ArtScroll/Schottenstein English Talmud (1990). Rav Pam was very pleased with the draft and urged that the project go forward.

All sorts of questions were brought to his door. When an organization was founded to provide a daily means of transportation for the infirm and the elderly in the New York area, Rav Pam was asked if the name *Ki B'Simchah Seitzei'u* (For With Gladness They Go Out) would be appropriate. Rav Pam replied, "The name is excellent, except that it will be a problem when a person needs to be driven to a funeral. A van bearing the name *Ki B'Smichah Seitzei'u* would be inappropriate at such a time." Rav Pam suggested the name *Rodeph Chesed* ("Pursuer of Kindness"), and that is what the organization is called.

Peaceful Solutions I

When products manufactured by the Lenoxx electronics company appeared in the holiday catalog of some chain department stores, this did not sit very well with the people at Lenox China. They contacted the co-owners of Lenoxx, R' Berish and R' Moshe Fuchs, and demanded that they change their company's name. The brothers saw this as an unreasonable demand, as the two companies' logos were different, the names were spelled differently, and their merchandise was different! Lenox China sued and a court date was set.

(left to right): Moshe and Berish Fuchs holding the mantle that they dedicated to adorn the sefer Torah written in honor of their rebbi, Rav Pam

The day before the hearing, the Fuchs brothers went to their rebbi, Rav Pam, to receive his *berachah*. He readily obliged and also offered some advice. "Why not add something to your company's name so that the other company will be satisfied? Since your company specializes in audio equipment, why not call yourselves 'Lenoxx Sound'?" The suggestion seemed to be a good one, but the brothers could not give it much thought with the court hearing taking place on the following day.

At the hearing, the judge was clearly annoyed. "I don't see the problem; one company sells china, the other sells electronics. When Lenox China will go into the electronics business, we'll have a case on our hands." Then, he turned to the lawyer representing the Fuchs brothers and said, "Why don't you resolve this peacefully by adding something to your company's name? Why not call it 'Lenoxx Sound'?"

And that is the company's name to this day.

Peaceful Solutions II

Every year during *Aseres Yemei Teshuvah*, a parlor meeting to benefit Yeshivah and Mesivta Torah Vodaath was held in Queens. The highlight was an address by the Rosh HaYeshivah, Rav Pam.

One year, after Torah Vodaath had already scheduled its parlor meeting, a well-known organization announced that it would be having a parlor meeting on the same night in the same neighborhood. Its meeting would also be graced by the presence of one of the *gedolei hador*. The organizers of the Torah Vodaath event immediately contacted this organization and asked that they reschedule their meeting for another night. While the organization's director was apologetic, he said that with so many days taken up by Yom Tov, there was no other day for the event that was satisfactory.

The Torah Vodaath organizers approached Rav Pam. Perhaps, they suggested, if pressure were applied, the organization would give in and reschedule. Rav Pam did not agree to this. Instead, he advised that the Torah Vodaath parlor meeting begin earlier than originally planned, and the organization's parlor meeting be scheduled for a later hour.

At the annual Queens parlor meeting:
Rav Pam with the meeting's host Yisroel Blumenfrucht and sons.

This would solve the problem. The organization was contacted and agreed to Rav Pam's suggestion.

At the Torah Vodaath meeting, Rav Pam began his remarks by thanking everyone for coming despite the early hour. He explained that the time had been changed because an organization, which he named, would be having its own parlor meeting later that evening. He went on to speak the praises of that organization and said that it was most worthy of everyone's support! Only after this introduction did he speak about Torah Vodaath.

People were amazed. Had Rav Pam insisted, the organization very possibly would have postponed its parlor meeting. Instead, Rav Pam had proposed a solution that satisfied everyone. To go yet further and use his speech to encourage support of that organization was certainly most unusual.

Someone remarked, "Rav Pam was going in the way of his rebbi, Reb Shraga Feivel Mendlowitz. To Reb Shraga Feivel, there was no such thing as 'my yeshivah' and 'your yeshivah,' 'my organization' and 'your organization.' Everything was for the sake of Hashem and His Torah, and therefore all causes were important and worthy of his support."

Learning from Stories

Rav Pam knew a wealth of stories involving *gedolei Yisrael* of previous generations. At times, the advice he offered was based on a lesson he had learned from a particular story.

Someone posed the following question: He presently held a low-ranking but well-paying position with a successful New York firm. He had recently been offered the post of Chief Executive Officer of a new company which would be opening outside of New York, in a city with a large Torah community. There was the possibility that he could eventually become a part-owner of the company and have his sons succeed him upon his retirement. Should he accept the position?

Rav Pam said he should remain where he was. His current salary provided his family with all their needs. Spiritually, he and his family were doing well; he attended *shiurim* and devoted a significant portion of his time to learning. Why tamper with success?

He then related the following:

Two men approached Rabbi Yosef Dov Soloveitchik, author of *Beis HaLevi*, with the identical question: Should they uproot themselves and their families and emigrate to America where the prospects of earning a living were far greater than in 19th-century Lithuania?

The Beis HaLevi told one man to make the move; the other he advised to remain in Lithuania. When the second man asked for an explanation, the Beis HaLevi said: "When we say *Hallel* on Succos, we shake the *lulav* when saying the words אָנָּא ה' הוֹשִׁיעָה נָּא *(Please, Hashem, save us now!)*, but not when we say אָנָּא ה' הַצְלִיחָה נָּא *(Please, Hashem, grant us success now!)*. This hints to something: When we need a *'yeshuah'* (salvation), we need to 'shake' (i.e. uproot) ourselves and move elsewhere if necessary. But one should not 'shake' himself merely to seek greater success.

"The other man is finding it impossible to provide for his family here; he needs a *'yeshuah,'* so I told him to emigrate.

You, however, are providing for your family's needs; what you seek is greater success. It is better for you to remain here."

Kosher Kitchens

A dedicated group in Brooklyn arranged for a number of non-religious families to receive weekly food packages so that they would be able to eat kosher food. Then, some of these families were seen in a local supermarket, purchasing non-kosher meat. The immediate reaction of those involved was to stop sending the food packages, which were purchased from tzedakah funds. When Rav Pam was consulted, he responded with a story:

The Chofetz Chaim was the driving force behind the founding of kosher kitchens that provided food for Jewish soldiers in the Russian and Polish armies. Someone reported to the Chofetz Chaim that a number of soldiers were accepting the kosher food and also eating the standard non-kosher meals served by the army. The Chofetz Chaim responded that if that was the case, then the kosher kitchens should provide more and better food, for the more kosher food the soldiers ate, the less non-kosher food they were likely to eat.

Rav Pam concluded: Although these families were still purchasing non-kosher meat, it was worthwhile to continue to provide them with kosher food packages. The more kosher food they ate, the less non-kosher meat they would eat.

"I Counseled Well?"

A yeshivah student was graduating eighth grade and his parents could not decide which high school he

Addressing past and present talmidim at Mesivta Torah Vodaath.

should attend. Someone suggested to the father that he discuss the matter with Rav Pam. The man approached Rav Pam one morning in Torah Vodaath and, though they had never met before, Rav Pam graciously invited the man to come to his home to discuss the matter. At their meeting, the man explained his son's needs; after some discussion, Rav Pam said that a particular high school which the man had mentioned was best for his son.

Towards the end of the following school year, the man returned to Torah Vodaath to see Rav Pam. After being reminded of their meeting a year before, Rav Pam asked a bit anxiously, "So was my *eitzah* (advice) good? Was your son *matzliach* (successful)?" "Yes!," the man replied. "That is exactly why I have come, to thank the Rosh Yeshivah for his wonderful *eitzah*. My son is doing very well."

Rav Pam was overjoyed. He said, "On Yom Kippur, we say the *viduy* (confession) many times. When I pound my chest and say, 'יָעַצְנוּ רָע' (We have counseled evil), I have in mind the many times that I have counseled people. Who knows if I have advised them correctly? So when I meet someone whom I advised and I am told that יָעַצְתִּי טוֹב (I counseled well), it gives me great pleasure."

The Bottom Line

A former talmid came to Rav Pam to discuss a serious matter. After some discussion, Rav Pam offered his advice. As the talmid prepared to leave, he said, "Rebbi, in all honesty, I am still not at peace with the situation." Rav Pam replied, "Say to the *Ribono shel Olam*: חֲזֵי, דְּעָלָךְ קָא סָמְכִינָא *(See that I am relying on You — Bava Kamma* 100a)." The talmid was unfamiliar with this expression, so Rav Pam took a pen and paper and wrote it down for him. Years later, the talmid said, "I understood Rav Pam to mean that I was not to rely on his advice alone; for, after all is said and done, it is the *Ribono shel Olam* Who has to make the advice work.

"With this understanding, I was able to accept his advice with inner peace. Later, I took that piece of paper with the words ,חֲזֵי

דְעַלָךְ קָא סַמְכִינָא and placed it under a photograph of Rav Pam. To this day, those words continue to be a source of strength for me."

On another occasion Rav Pam said: "Everything we set out to accomplish requires *siyata diShmaya*. If when we go about our business, we strive to act according to Hashem's will, we then have a right to say חַזֵי, דְעַלָךְ קָא סַמְכִינָא."

רבש״ע, חזי דעלך קא סמיכנא!

The words that continue to inspire.

CHAPTER FIFTEEN

Rav Pam's Special Friend

In the winter of 1989, a son was born to Rabbi and Mrs. Baruch Rabinowitz of Ditmas Park, Brooklyn. The child, to be named Nota Shlomo, was born with Down Syndrome.

Rav Pam was Nota Shlomo's *sandak*. In the years that followed, Rav Pam developed a deep attachment to the child. When Nota Shlomo was past the age of four, his father began taking him to shul on Shabbos. Nota Shlomo did not disturb the davening; instead, he would circle the perimeter of the

As sandak at Nota Shlomo's bris

Torah Vodaath beis midrash with quick steps, again and again. Someone suggested that perhaps this was not in keeping with *kevod hatefillah* (respect for prayer). Rav Pam disagreed. "Perhaps this is his way of davening," he said, for he understood that Nota Shlomo possesses a special *neshamah*. "If it's not really disturbing, we should not stop him."

Sometimes during davening, Nota Shlomo would place himself to the right of the *Aron Kodesh* with a Tehillim in hand and shake to and fro, lift both his hands upward, say the *pasuk* of *Shema Yisrael* and make other sounds as if he were davening. Rav Pam mentioned this in a shmuess to his talmidim and commented that one cannot know what such a child accomplishes with his "tefillah." Similarly, when Nota Shlomo hurried to open the *Aron Kodesh* before *krias HaTorah*, Rav Pam remarked that certainly it was of great importance for the minyan that he was the one performing this honor.

For a few years, Nota Shlomo's standard greeting to everyone in shul was, "*Gut Shabbos* — what name?" The first few times he greeted Rav Pam this way, the tzaddik responded, "*Gut Shabbos*, Nota Shlomo; my name is Avraham." Nota Shlomo then said, "*Gut Shabbos*, Avraham," which, of course, was embarrassing to Rabbi Rabinowitz.

One day, Rabbi Rabinowitz showed his son a picture of Rav Pam and asked him, "Who is this?" When Nota Shlomo responded, "Avraham," his father said, "No, this is *Rav Pam*." They practiced saying "Rav Pam," a number of times, after which Rabbi Rabinowitz told his son, "So next time you say '*Gut Shabbos,*' it's, '*Gut Shabbos*, Rav Pam.' "

The next Shabbos, when Rav Pam said, "*Gut Shabbos*, Nota Shlomo, my name is Avraham," Nota Shlomo responded, "No, not Avraham — *Rav Pam!*" Rav Pam laughed and with genuine happiness exclaimed, "Oh, he is a smart one!" Rabbi Rabinowitz recalls that Rav Pam looked for every opportunity to point out Nota Shlomo's progress and to praise him for his accomplishments.

A Heavenly Sign

Rav Pam became seriously ill in the winter of 1997 and underwent major surgery. On the seventh day of the Pesach that followed, Rav Pam davened, as usual, at Torah Vodaath.

Everyone, including Nota Shlomo, knew not to disturb Rav Pam during davening and *krias HaTorah*. If someone wanted to speak to Rav Pam, he would wait until the conclusion of davening. Thus, it was very unusual when on that Pesach morning, Nota

Shlomo approached Rav Pam between *aliyos* during the Torah reading, shook his hand, and then pointed to a *shtender* (lectern) nearby. On the *shtender* were two *sefarim* and what appeared to be a pamphlet. Thinking that the child wanted to hold a *sefer*, Rav Pam picked one up and tried to hand it to Nota Shlomo. But Nota Shlomo shook his head, "No!" after which Rav Pam tried to hand him the second *sefer*, but again Nota Shlomo refused to accept it. Rav Pam then held out the pamphlet to Nota Shlomo, who accepted it, smiled and handed it back to Rav Pam, who placed it back on the *shtender*.

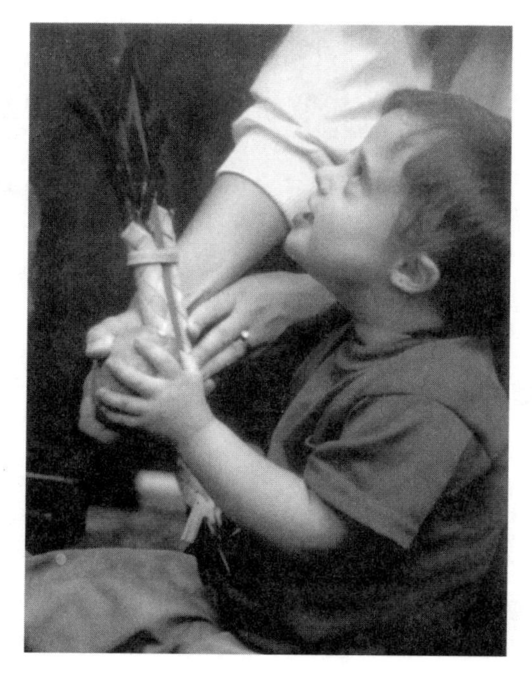

Nota Shlomo was obviously unhappy with this and exclaimed, "No, no, no!" The entire scenario was repeated again with Nota Shlomo refusing to accept each of the two *sefarim*, and finally accepting the pamphlet. This time, the child pointed to the pamphlet before handing it back to Rav Pam. At this point, Rav Pam smiled broadly and patted Nota Shlomo's hand as if to thank him, and left the pamphlet on his own shtender. After davening, someone asked Rav Pam, "What was Nota Shlomo trying to show the Rosh Yeshivah?" Rav Pam preferred not to explain.

A few months later on a summer morning, Rabbi Rabinowitz approached Rav Pam after Shacharis to discuss something.

As he began to walk away when the conversation ended, Rav Pam said: "Your Nota Shlomo is so precious — I have to tell you a story that happened with him." Rav Pam proceeded to relate what had happened on the morning of the seventh day of Pesach. He then explained:

> *When I took ill this winter, I decided to undertake an additional study session as a zechus (source of merit) for a refuah (healing). I was undecided as to what I should study. My choices were: a masechta of Gemara; a seder of Mishnah; or the Chofetz Chaim's works on shemiras halashon. Each choice had an advantage that the other two did not.*
>
> *For weeks, I could not decide this matter. I was determined to make a decision by the close of the seventh day of Pesach. On that morning in the beis midrash, Nota Shlomo refused the two sefarim that I offered him — but he happily accepted the pamphlet, which was the yearly calendar for the study of the Chofetz Chaim's sefarim on shemiras halashon! The second time, Nota Shlomo even pointed to the Chofetz Chaim's picture on the cover before handing it back. I took this as a sign from Hashem of what I should choose to study: the Chofetz Chaim's works on shemiras halashon.*

"You should know," Rav Pam concluded, "that as a result of my decision, the talmidim of our beis medrash and of Beis Medrash Elyon (in Monsey) have also undertaken the study of *shemiras halashon* — and this is all because of Nota Shlomo."

Rejoicing with the Torah

For most Down Syndrome children, singing and dancing have special meaning. For Nota Shlomo, Simchas Torah is a highlight of the year. When Nota Shlomo was almost eight years old, his grandparents bought him a child's *sefer Torah* to hold on Simchas Torah. Throughout the night and day in shul, he held the Torah tightly, displaying an unusual attachment to it. Only with great encouragement did he put down the *sefer Torah* from time to time and dance.

On the morning of Simchas Torah when the Torah reading began in the beis medrash of Torah Vodaath, Nota Shlomo approached the *gabbai* at the *bimah* and offered him his *sefer Torah* to use for the Torah reading. The *gabbai* politely refused the offer, but Nota Shlomo continued to ask that his *sefer Torah* be used. And though his father instructed him to return to his seat, the child returned to the *bimah* a number of times to again make his request. Finally, Rabbi Rabinowitz told his son quietly but firmly that the *gabbai* would not use his *sefer Torah*, and that he should return to his seat and sit nicely.

Rav Pam, who was sitting in his regular seat only a few feet away from the *bimah*, overheard this. He motioned for Nota Shlomo to come over to him. Rav Pam spoke to the child in a whisper for less than a minute and succeeded in calming him. Nota Shlomo happily returned to his seat. When Mussaf got underway, Nota Shlomo became a bit anxious, and every few minutes he asked his father how much time was left until the end of davening.

As soon as davening ended, Nota Shlomo said, "*Abba*, now my turn." He then took his *sefer Torah* to the *bimah*, put it down and said, "Rav Pam said now my turn."

Rabbi Rabinowitz approached Rav Pam, who explained, "I told Nota Shlomo that right now we are using the big *sefer Torah*, but after davening we would do more *leining* from *his sefer Torah* and that we will call up people to the Torah."

And so after most people had left, Nota Shlomo's *sefer Torah* was opened on the *bimah* of Mesivta Torah Vodaath and, with

some 15 people crowded around the *bimah*, three people were called up by name for their *"aliyos."* After each man pretended to recite the blessing over the Torah, Nota Shlomo, standing on a chair, proudly "read" from his *sefer Torah*. When the third *"aliyah"* was completed, two men were honored with *"hagbahah"* and *"gelilah."* Then, the *sefer Torah* was given to Nota Shlomo and everyone joined in a lively dance.

One Shabbos afternoon, Nota Shlomo walked home from Pirchei groups alone, which involved crossing three streets. His parents were very concerned, especially when they spoke to him and he insisted that he *was* "big enough" to cross streets by himself.

His father told him, "Nota Shlomo, whenever we have an important question, we ask Rav Pam what to do. We're going to Rav Pam and he will *pasken* (decide) whether or not you are old enough to cross the street alone."

They came to Rav Pam and Rabbi Rabinowitz said, "Nota Shlomo feels that he is big enough to cross the street by himself, but his parents feel that he should not cross. What does the Rosh Yeshivah say?"

Rav Pam smiled and took the child's hand in his own. "Nota Shlomo, you are *very big*," he said kindly, "but in order to cross the street, you must be even bigger. *Im yirtzeh Hashem* (G-d willing), the time will come when you will be able to cross the street alone — but not yet."

Nota Shlomo accepted Rav Pam's decision happily and said, "Thank you." From that day on, if someone asked Nota Shlomo if he crossed the street by himself, he replied, "Rav Pam said, 'No!' "

"Rav Pam Misses Him"

As already mentioned, the last years of Rav Pam's life, when walking was very difficult for him, a minyan would gather in his house for all the tefillos of Shabbos and Yom Tov. Rabbi Rabinowitz would bring Nota Shlomo for Minchah on Shabbos afternoon and Rav Pam would always seat the boy to his left. If someone else was already occupying the seat when the Rabinowitzes walked in, Rav Pam would have Nota Shlomo stand next to him. Rav Pam would greet Nota Shlomo with a hug and the child would always ask, "How's Rav Pam?"

As time went on, the size of the minyan grew to the point that the overcrowdedness in the Pams' small dining room area made it stuffy and unhealthy for a man in Rav Pam's condition. With great reluctance, Rav Pam permitted a family member to hang up a sign on the front door which stated:

> *Though the Rosh Yeshivah would love to have everyone join the minyan, his medical condition no longer allows for it. If this sign is hanging, it means that there is already a minyan inside and everyone is requested to daven at one of the good battei midrash in the neighborhood.*

As a result, Rabbi Rabinowitz no longer came to Minchah — until he was contacted by Rav Pam's devoted grandson, R' Binyamin.

"My grandfather made it clear from the outset," he said, "that the 'regulars' at the minyan should continue coming even if they see the sign hanging. And my grandfather misses Nota Shlomo. He misses seeing him and he misses the *simchah* that

Nota Shlomo brings to him. So please make sure to bring Nota Shlomo along."

The following Shabbos afternoon, when Nota Shlomo entered the Pam residence, he ran straight for Rav Pam, grabbed hold of his legs and hugged him. And Rav Pam responded in kind, holding Nota Shlomo close to him. Someone attemped to get the child away, for instructions had been given that to prevent any passing of germs, no one was to shake Rav Pam's hand. But Rav Pam told the person, "For him [Nota Shlomo], it's okay."

Nota Shlomo let go, took a step back and noticed how visibly ill Rav Pam appeared. (He had been discharged from the hospital only a few days earlier.) "Why Rav Pam so weak?" he wanted to know. "Why am I so weak?" Rav Pam responded softly, a slight smile on his lips. "What do I know? Ask the *Ribono shel Olam*." Rav Pam, of course, did not mean to complain. He *never* complained. He meant that Hashem does everything for a reason, though we do not always know the reason.

Nota Shlomo looked upwards and said, "Hashem, why Rav Pam so weak? Make him all better. Give him *refuah sheleimah*!"

Rav Pam took hold of the boy and said with emotion, "Nota Shlomo, may Hashem answer your tefillos and grant us both a *refuah sheleimah*, so that we can together go to greet *Mashiach tzidkeinu, bimheirah v'yameinu, Amein.*"

In June, when Rav Pam was again hospitalized, Nota Shlomo drew a picture of someone in bed and wrote, "Dear Rav Pam, feel all better, *refuah sheleimah*. Love, Shlomo." When the letter arrived in the mail, Rebbetzin Pam brought it to Rav Pam and read it to him. Rav Pam remarked that Nota Shlomo brought him tremendous joy. He instructed his grandson to inform Nota Shlomo that he had received the letter and that he appreciated it. "But tell him," he said, "that his name is not Shlomo — it is *Nota* Shlomo."

The morning of Rav Pam's funeral, by which time the Rabinowitz family had heard the tragic news, Rabbi Rabinowitz arrived home from Shacharis to find Nota Shlomo sitting on the porch. He said, "Rav Pam sick, Rav Pam hospital, Rav Pam died. Now Rav Pam happy." He then marched into the house, grabbed a Chumash and said, "Me learn Chumash for Rav Pam." Each day of *shivah,* he sat for a while learning Chumash — and to this day, when he remembers, he learns Chumash for Rav Pam's *neshamah.*

CHAPTER SIXTEEN

Final Years

In 1997, Rav Pam learned that he had a serious illness, and would have to undergo major surgery. The original prognosis was quite bleak. Rav Pam reacted to the news with unshakable *emunah* (faith in Hashem). He said, "I am not depressed at all. ה׳ הוּא הַטּוֹב בְּעֵינָיו יַעֲשֶׂה (He is Hashem; He will do what is good in His eyes — *I Shmuel* 3:18). I feel great *hakaras hatov* to the *Ribono shel Olam*."

A few weeks prior to the surgery, Rav Pam had been asked to serve as *kohen* at a group *pidyon haben* for some ten first-

In the fall of 1996, when Rav Pam was 83 years old, the sefer Torah written in his honor was dedicated. Here the completed sefer Torah is lifted, as Rav Pam and those assembled clap and sing.

born boys from the former Soviet Union. Rav Pam attended the *pidyon haben*. He brought with him beautifully polished silver coins to give each of the boys as a remembrance of that special event in their lives.

The next day, he entered the hospital in preparation for surgery. On that morning, R' Avraham Biderman visited R' Pam at Mesivta Torah Vodaath and then drove him home. As they were preparing to leave the yeshivah, Rav Pam said, "Avraham, find me a *zechus*, something that I can do." Mr. Biderman was a bit taken aback by this request. "Rebbi doesn't need me to tell him what he should do." "No, no," Rav Pam responded, "I need *zechusim*."

> *They left the building and started to walk down the block when Rav Pam said that he had to return to the yeshivah, and abruptly turned around. They entered the lobby of the yeshivah,*

where a Hispanic maintenance worker was mopping the floor. "Good morning," said a smiling Rav Pam. The worker returned the greeting and Rav Pam left the building. "I always say 'Good morning' to him," Rav Pam told Mr. Biderman. "But I was so preoccupied with my thoughts that I did not greet him when we left the first time."

After the surgery, the doctors were much more hopeful, though they informed Rav Pam that his condition would require treatments. Rav Pam reacted to this news with happiness and gratitude to Hashem. Eight days after the surgery, a talmid visited Rav Pam at the hospital and found him in excellent spirits, sitting up and studying the weekly *parashah*. They discussed Torah topics and then the conversation turned to Rav Pam's condition. "Whatever will be will be," he said. "If I must endure *yisurim* (afflictions), that is also good." And he continued to radiate genuine happiness.

For the rest of his life, he was almost always in pain. Nevertheless, he succeeded in concealing this from everyone except those closest to him. He explained, "I don't want to cause others *agmas nefesh* (distress)." And while his family knew that he was in pain, he rarely spoke about it. When asked directly, "Are you in pain?" he would often reply, "*Morgen vet zein besser* (Tomorrow will be better)."

Once, when a talmid asked how he was feeling, Rav Pam replied, "מַה יִּתְאוֹנֵן אָדָם חַי — How can a person who is alive complain?[1] *He should be happy just to be alive."*

---

1. *Eichah* 3:39.

In his last years, it was difficult for Rav Pam to attend simchas of talmidim, so Rabbi Zev Smith brought his son's bar mitzvah celebration to Rav Pam's home.

When someone asked Rav Pam how he distracted himself during treatments, which sometimes lasted a few hours, he replied, "I review *mishnayos baal peh* (by heart)."

In the fall of 2000, after undergoing cataract surgery, he asked a grandson to come to his house to learn with him. He explained that with one eye covered by a post-operative patch and the other eye in need of the same surgery, he could not study from a *sefer*. "I've memorized *perakim* of Mishnayos in various *masechtos* so that I can learn on walks and when I go for treatments. But now [because of weakness], I get 'stuck' every now and then." Having said that, he began to review *Mishnayos Rosh Hashanah* and, with his grandson's help, he completed the *masechta*.

At one point, he was in constant, extreme pain except when lying down. He lay in bed for hours, awake for much of the time. When Rav Pam's son, R' Asher, found him learning in his study for a short while, R' Asher was surprised that he had gotten out of bed at all. "One cannot stay in bed all day and not accomplish anything," Rav Pam explained. "I'm learning one of Reb Akiva Eiger's *teshuvos* (responsa). This way I will have something to think about when I return to bed."

With Others in Mind

When leaving his house for the hospital to undergo surgery, Rav Pam took with him a new book he had received containing stories of Torah leaders. He explained, "I know that family members will be visiting me and there will be times when I will be sleeping or simply unable to speak with my visitors. I don't want them to be bored so I brought this along for them to read."

Until he was physically unable to do so, he would visit other patients whenever he was hospitalized.

Once, when he entered a doctor's office to undergo treatment, a woman who also was a patient asked that he bless her. Rav Pam said, "*Der Eibershter hot lieb Yiddishe techter* (Hashem loves Jewish daughters)," and he offered her his blessing for a complete recovery. Then, he turned to the other patients in the room — Jews and non-Jews — and he wished them all a speedy return to full health. His words, which flowed straight from the heart, left a deep impression upon everyone.

During Rav Pam's last, pain-filled years, Rebbetzin Pam, his children and grandchildren did their best to guard his health, while allowing others to consult with him as much as was possible.

One day, Rebbetzin Pam met one of Rav Pam's former talmidim who, she knew, had suffered a personal tragedy. "Why have you stopped visiting?" she wanted to know. "I know that Rebbi is not well," the young man replied, "and I don't feel right bothering him."

"Whether or not Rabbi Pam is feeling well is my concern," the Rebbetzin replied. "You should try to visit, and I'll decide whether or not it's a good time."

Chesed Amid Pain

During this period, Rav Pam became involved with performing *chesed* as never before. Hundreds of thousands of dollars in tzedakah funds passed through his hands. Rav Pam said that often his pain made it difficult for him to concentrate on intensive learning. At such times, he would use the gift of life for *chesed*, which could be done without mental strain.

> *Rav Pam's family became concerned that the flow of visitors and callers was too much of a strain for him, and would further weaken his health. Someone suggested that he should have one day "off" each week to allow his body to rest. Rav Pam, frail and bent, rejected the suggestion. "What if someone needs me for something urgent on that day? This is not an option."*

One night, he received a call from a teenager living with relatives away from home, who was very unhappy with his situation. "I have no friends," the boy remarked sadly. "You have one friend for sure," came the reply, "Avraham Pam."

As their conversation continued, the possibility was mentioned that the boy move out of his relatives' home. "You could come here," Rav Pam suggested. Later, someone asked Rav Pam if he truly thought it was possible to take the boy into his home at that time. Rav Pam responded with a story:

When the great *gaon* and *tzaddik* Rabbi Isser Zalman Meltzer was old and weak, a woman approached him and asked that he write a letter in Russian for her. Someone asked him, "Has the Rav become a secretary in his old age?"

R' Isser Zalman replied, "What does the *Ribono shel Olam* have from me now that I do not have the strength to learn, if not that I should do a little *chesed*?"

Lieutenant Richardson

Lieutenant Steven Richardson of the New York City Police Department was a longtime neighbor of Rav Pam and, as a registered nurse, attended Rav Pam with great devotion from the time he took ill in 1997 until his passing. In his words:

> *I never met a patient like Rabbi Pam. He never, ever complained, never winced. He could not have been more gracious. Despite his illness and pain, he tried to help his students and the community as much as possible. Had it been up to him, he would have given and given until he couldn't speak. But his wife watched over him unbelievably and did her best to protect his health.*
>
> *As a Lieutenant in the 66th precinct, I came to realize how much clout Rabbi Pam's name carried in the community. He was always grateful to me and would often ask me if there was any way that*

Lieutenant Steven Richardson greeting Rav Pam at the start of the hachnasas Sefer Torah celebration in 1996.

he could help me with my career in the police department or as a nurse. I declined the offer but I was touched by it.

My first responsibility in caring for him was to flush a tube that was connected to him. This was not pleasant for him, but he handled it with grace and humor. Later, he needed to undergo treatments which left him thoroughly drained; he was absolutely exhausted. Yet, he was always upbeat and, to my amazement, he continued to meet with people in his study and even returned to his yeshivah.

He developed severe spinal problems; his spine became extremely brittle. He was in constant, excruciating pain. He underwent spinal fusion, and then had to practice walking again. I saw how determined he was. He began by walking across his living room to his kitchen. He counted the steps he took out loud, "One ... two ... " This was to be his accomplishment at that time. Later he was able to walk down the block, and eventually he could walk all the way to yeshivah. Truthfully, I had not believed that he would ever be able to return to his work at the school, but he did.

From the time that he developed spinal problems, he walked in the street pushing a shopping cart to maintain balance. He once told me that he wanted to conceal his pain and illness from the community, "because they won't come to me if they know that I am sick." I believe that this is why he used a shopping cart and not a walker, which is the common device used in such cases. He felt that a walker would make his illness more obvious and would discourage people from seeking his help.

There were times when he counseled people while confined to bed. He just kept on going, doing whatever he could do until almost the very end, when he told me one day, "I'm really worn out."

His mind remained sharp to the very end. He understood quite well how seriously ill he was, but he did not let this affect his spirits. He was concerned only that others should not be distressed over his condition.

His Final Year

In the last year of his life, Rav Pam's condition worsened considerably. Despite frailty, extreme weakness and ever-present discomfort, he pushed himself to the limits of his physical abilities to assist others.

On Simchas Torah that year, some 25 men and boys gathered in his home for the morning davening and *hakafos*. It was announced that to minimize the strain on the Rosh Yeshivah, the Torah portion would be read only once when five men would be called to the Torah; everyone else would have to make their way to Torah Vodaath after Mussaf to fulfill the custom of being called to the Torah on Simchas Torah.

Rav Pam objected. Whoever came to his minyan on this day had come expecting to be called to the Torah. It was not right to ask them to go to the yeshivah for their *aliyah*.

After some discussion, a "compromise" was reached. All married men would be called to the Torah in Rav Pam's home, while all bachurim would go to the yeshivah. *"Zeit mir mochel* (Please forgive me)," Rav Pam asked of the bachurim. He stood throughout the entire Torah reading.

In the fall of 2000, his condition worsened and he was extremely weak. For a while, Rav Pam was unable to be in yeshivah, but in Kislev he regained some of his strength and he resumed coming to yeshivah for Shacharis, and delivering *shiurim* and *shmuessen*. Then, he was plagued by kidney problems and doctors ordered him to lie in bed with his feet

Rav Pam, in his final years, with his lifelong friend Rav Nesanel Quinn, after Shacharis in Torah Vodaath.

elevated. He continued to learn Torah to whatever degree was humanly possible. When he was hospitalized, and studying from a *sefer* became impossible, he learned from memory.

One day, some young men arrived from Eretz Yisrael with a sorrowful tale. Their distinguished father had taken ill; as a result, their family was faced with astronomical debts, and the bank threatened to seize their parents' possessions.

Rav Pam personally raised $40,000 for this family.

A Doctor's View

Dr. Robert Schulman cared for Rav Pam with great devotion during this difficult period. He recalled:

> *Rav Pam was a remarkable person. He handled himself very nobly throughout his illness. Though he was in a lot of pain, he bore it graciously and almost never complained.*

When he was hospitalized during the last two months of his life, there was a "No Visitors" sign on his door. Nevertheless, there were other patients who would come to visit him. He greeted them kindly and wished them "refuah sheleimah."

Even at that difficult time, he was preoccupied with Shuvu. His involvement with Shuvu was a refuah (healing) for him. When those involved with Shuvu would visit him, he displayed a genuine interest in what was happening within the organization. They would read letters from Shuvu children and his spirits would soar. It was something miraculous.

He was very bright, very strong, so modest and so humble. He was very special, and at the same time, he had no airs about him.

His way was one of "menschlichkeit." He was polite to everyone. One day, when he and his wife came to my office for an appointment, Rebbetzin Pam gave my Irish medical assistant a warm, personal congratulations on the birth of her twins. My gentile office staff was amazed that the rebbetzin showed such warmth to someone of another religion. They sometimes complain that their own Jewish neighbors do not greet them with a "Good morning" when they see them on the street. But Rav Pam was not like this.

In the hospital, the nurses were totally devoted to him. They respected both him and his family. He was always very polite and never demanding.

He was very careful with his speech. He spoke a "king's English," and this included following the rules of English grammar. In his last days, when hospitalized, he overheard a young grandchild tell someone, "There's apples in the refrigerator." Rav Pam called the child to his bedside and said, "There ***are*** *apples in the refrigerator."*

"I'm So Grateful"

During one of his last hospital stays, a doctor became a bit frustrated because Rav Pam was not letting anyone know when he was in pain. "You don't *have to* be in pain," the doctor told him. "If you're in pain, tell us and we'll get you two Tylenol." That night, his grandson said, "Zeidy, some things we can't help, but there's no reason why we can't try to ease your pain. All you have to do is complain a little bit and we'll know that you're in pain."

Rav Pam became very serious and responded, "Binyamin, do you know how old I am? — 88. Do you know how old 88 is? It's a long time. Some people don't live until 50. Fewer people live until 60, even less until 70 or 80. Look at what the *Ribono shel Olam* gave me — 88 years! I'm so *makir tov* (grateful) for this! So, if along with those years comes some pain, you want me to complain about it? How can I complain?"

On a Friday in June, Rav Pam suddenly lapsed into a semi-coma and was rushed to Maimonides Medical Center. Anxious family members stood at his bedside speaking to him, but he did not respond. When a talmid arrived, a family member said to him, "We don't know if he hears us or not, but try talking to him. Tell him something about yeshivah."

The talmid bent down and said that he still remembered

the very first shmuess which he had heard from his Rebbi. It centered around a mishnah in *Masechta Eduyos* which, said the talmid, listed five ways in which a father benefits a son.

Suddenly, Rav Pam tried to say something. Everyone leaned forward trying to hear what he wanted to say. In his weakened state, it took him a few minutes to utter one word: "שִׁשָּׁה" *("Six")* and then he once again passed out.

In fact, the mishnah[2] lists *six* ways in which a father benefits a son, and it was this fact which Rav Pam had strained himself to say. It was a few hours before he regained full consciousness.

Meaningful Living

As soon as he was discharged from the hospital, Rav Pam said that he wanted to write a letter to one of our generation's great leaders, Rabbi Aharon Leib Steinman. Rav Pam had been informed that Rav Steinman had personally led the saying of Tehillim on his behalf, and he wanted to express his appreciation for this. However, he was too weak to write, so he dictated the letter to his grandson, R' Meir. He thanked Rav Steinman, adding that Rav Steinman's *davening* on his behalf meant a great deal to him — and he asked that he continue to daven for him. He closed with mazel tov wishes upon the marriage of Rav Steinman's grandchild.

Upon completing the letter, he told his grandson, "It would not be correct for you to sign my name to the letter," and he was too weak to sign personally. He thought for a moment and said to sign it (in Hebrew): "As heard from my grandfather and

2. *Eduyos* 2:9.

recorded by myself, Meir Pam."

He then told his grandson that while his life was now empty of pleasure because he could not learn Torah, it was worth living if he could still help another Jew in some way. That day, he received an overseas call from someone he knew. The man was unemployed and had already acted upon Rav Pam's advice that he should enter a job-training program. The man was calling now to say that he did not have money to continue his job training. Rav Pam had someone write down the details of the man's situation, in the hope that he would be able to assist him.

Welcoming Rabbi Aharon Leib Steinman to his home. R' Yitzchak Rosengarten of Bnei Brak, a trusted confidant of Rav Steinman, is in the background.

Rav Pam then asked his grandson to phone a close talmid, a man of wealth. He was too weak to hold the phone, so his grandson held it to his ear. "I need _______ dollars from you *today*," Rav Pam said. "Do this *chesed* for me and give me this amount." The talmid replied that he would send the money immediately, and Rav Pam's face shone with joy.

He then instructed his grandson to phone a needy individual and ask that he come to see him. When the man arrived some ten minutes later, Rav Pam handed him a check for $1800 and said, "Here is three months' rent." He then kissed the man's hand and blessed him. The man was overjoyed. When he left, Rav Pam was extremely happy. "Today was an accomplished day! Now I can lie down."

Two Requests

He told his grandson R' Binyamin that in his last years he constantly beseeched Hashem that he be granted two requests: that his mind should remain clear until the end of his life, and that the tzedakah funds which he raised should be distributed to *aniyim hagunim*, worthy poor people.

> *During that period, Rav Pam remarked, "Never in my life did I ever become depressed. Whatever happens to me is because the Ribono shel Olam wants it to happen. I'm not going to get upset if this is what Hashem wants.*
>
> *"I'm a realist; at my age, I expect to be sick. I'm not going to become depressed. When a person reaches a certain age, the body begins to weaken. Ten years ago, I was amazed at how healthy I was."*

In his last years, he would express the hope that he would live to wear the *kohen's* clothing in the *Beis HaMikdash* and perform the *avodah*. On the Fast of the 17th of Tammuz, as he lay ill and alarmingly weak, his family sat around his bed, searching for something to say that would stimulate him. When a grandson said, "Zeide, soon it will be time to put on the *bigdei kehunah (kohen's* clothing) and perform the service on the *mizbei'ach* (altar)," his face lit up.

His Last Parlor Meeting

The annual Shuvu summer parlor meeting, at the home of R' Gedaliah Weinberger, was scheduled, as usual, in the year 2001. Rav Pam, recently discharged from the hospital, was pitifully weak and but a shadow of his former self. A hospital bed had been installed on the ground floor of his house and he needed assistance with every activity, including putting on his tallis and tefillin.

It seemed that it would be physically impossible for him to attend the parlor meeting. Yet Rav Pam was determined to attend this important fundraiser, for he knew that his presence would help raise more funds, funds that would mean another Shuvu school, another summer program, another battalion of youngsters in the army of Torah life.

Dr. Schulman approved of Rav Pam attending the meeting, for he had seen firsthand how Rav Pam drew strength from his

At one of the last Shuvu dinners of Rav Pam's life: (left to right) Rav Pam, Rabbi Aharon Schechter, Rabbi Aryeh Malkiel Kotler

involvement with Shuvu. With Rebbetzin Pam's understanding and approval, the arrangements were made. On the night before the meeting, Rav Pam related the speech he had prepared to Dr. Schulman. But in the morning he said that he would not be giving that speech. Apparently, he realized that his extreme weakness would prevent him from saying more than a few words. All day, he lay in bed in silence, conserving his strength. When Rabbi Chaim Michoel Gutterman, who had just arrived from Eretz Yisrael, came to see Rav Pam, all he could manage to say was, "Where are we opening new schools?"

Getting dressed was itself a painful process and took about an hour. Rav Pam was brought to the Weinberger home in a hospital bed, accompanied by Dr. Schulman and Hatzolah volunteers. The bed was carried into the house, to an area partitioned off by curtains, and placed near the podium. Rav Pam was carefully lifted into a chair which was then pulled up to a table. The curtains were parted. He spoke for about five minutes, which itself was incredible, considering that throughout the day he had barely said a word. But more than words, his mere presence delivered a powerful message: If Rav Pam could undertake such physical pain and hardship for the sake of Shuvu, should not everyone show some self-sacrifice by pledging money beyond their means for the Shuvu children? When the meeting ended and the pledges were counted, it was clear that the evening had been an overwhelming success.

The next morning, Rabbi Gutterman and R' Avraham Biderman visited Rav Pam. Apparently his participation in the parlor meeting had injected him with a bit of strength. Whereas on the previous day he had barely uttered a word, he was now able to speak more. While lying in bed, Rav Pam asked for a full report of the meeting's results. He told his visitors that he was saving the remainder of his prepared speech for the next Shuvu dinner.

❧

At the summer parlor meeting held one year after Rav Pam's passing, the Lakewood *Mashgiach*, Rabbi Matisyahu Salomon, reflected:

> *I was here last year when the Rosh Yeshivah,* זֵכֶר צַדִּיק לִבְרָכָה*, was wheeled in on a stretcher. They put up partitions, but we were able to see how painful it was, how difficult it was. And I was becoming angrier and angrier. Who had decided that it was permissible to wear out a gadol's last energies for a parlor meeting? I was determined to find out who was responsible for this and admonish them.*
>
> *I investigated and learned that the only one responsible for Rav Pam being there was Rav Pam. My anger turned to amazement. I thought of the pain, the inconvenience, the discomfort, of the embarrassment at being unable to fully express oneself. And my amazement turned to admiration.*
>
> *This was a final lesson in mesiras nefesh (self-sacrifice). Rav Pam understood that his presence would make a difference so he made the effort, the sacrifice.*

Final Days

Rav Pam spent the final weeks of his life in Boro Park's Maimonides Medical Center. Many talmidim, perhaps hundreds, passed through the hospital room to offer a tefillah for their rebbi.

A nurse was especially moved by the emotions of one man, who was davening with particular feeling. As he was leaving, she asked him, "What are you to Rabbi Pam?"

"Grateful," he responded.

Rabbi Yisroel Reisman was among the many who were present when Rav Pam left this world. In his words:

> *Rav Pam was surrounded by a few dozen talmidim, who had been davening at his side for the last six hours of his life. As the end drew closer and the appropriate tefillos were completed, Shema Yisrael ... was recited. At* אֶחָד*, the verse's concluding word, the heart monitor stopped. Rebbi had breathed his last.*
>
> *In recounting the death of Rabbi Akiva, Chazal state:* יָצְתָה נִשְׁמָתוֹ בְּאֶחָד*, his soul left him as he said the word "Echad."*[3] *In Rebbi's case, he was no longer conscious; it was the talmidim who had said "Echad." How fitting that this is how it was for our rebbi, whose life had revolved around his talmidim.*

The Funeral

The *levayah* (funeral) reflected the kind of humble tzaddik that Rav Pam was. If Rav Pam had been able to schedule his own *levayah*, he surely would have said that it should take place

3. *Berachos* 61b.

during *bein hazemanim* (intercession) so that yeshivah students would not lose time from their learning; on a Friday so that there would be little time to deliver *hespedim* (eulogies) and speak his praises; and during the summer when many people are away.

This is exactly what happened. This great and humble man, revered and cherished by so many, virtually slipped away. Some 20,000 people crowded the beis midrash of Torah Vodaath and the surrounding streets to bid a tearful farewell to perhaps the most beloved figure in the American yeshivah world, but there would have been many times that number if his passing had come on another day in another month. How fitting for a man whose fondest wish had always been to remain out of the spotlight, so that he could devote his life to learning and teaching.

Rav Pam had told his sons on a number of occasions that there should be no *hespedim* at his funeral. "I don't want to go to the World of Truth with a false passport," were his words. In his great humility, he was convinced that any praises said at his funeral would be exaggerations, and he desperately wanted to avoid this.

On one occasion, he told his son, R' Asher, "You know what they say of me while I'm alive — *nu*, what will they say of me then [i.e. at his funeral]? A *gaon* and a *tzaddik* — that's for sure! It's a *leitzanus* (a joke)! When they say such exaggerations I don't protest, because if I do, they will say that I'm an *anav* (a humble person) too! But I do protest when they compare me to the Chofetz Chaim — because that is a *bizayon* (disgrace) to the Chofetz Chaim." And Rav Pam proceeded to describe the Chofetz Chaim's greatness.

At his very brief funeral, a few chapters of Tehillim were recited, followed by a short farewell from his eldest son, R' Aharon. "אָבִי, אָבִי, (*My father, my father*)!" he cried, echoing the words used by the prophet Elisha when his rebbi, Eliyahu HaNavi, ascended Heavenward. "My father was a father to his children and a father to *Klal Yisrael*."

As his father would have wanted, R' Aharon expressed the family's deep gratitude to the physicians, members of Hatzolah, and talmidim, who showed such extraordinary devotion to Rav Pam during his final years.

Tombstone of Rav Pam. Note the hands at the top, spread as for Bircas Kohanim, and the date of his passing: 28 Av, 5761

He mentioned one other point. During Rav Pam's lifetime, he had involved himself with the needs of many individuals, who would have been lost without him. He dedicated himself to the education of Russian immigrant children, both in Eretz Yisrael and in America. In fact, shortly before his passing, Rav Pam expressed his anguish that two schools for Russian children in America were in danger of closing because of lack of funds — and with his last strength, he did everything he could to help keep these schools open.

It is vital, cried R' Aharon Pam, that his father's efforts not be forgotten and that everyone strive to help those whom he had helped with such self-sacrifice.

And the lessons of *midos* which he taught, in the classroom and by example, must never be forgotten.

The funeral procession then made its way down East Ninth Street and proceeded to Mount Judah Cemetery in Queens for burial.

A member of the Torah Vodaath kollel was in a used book store leafing through some books in the Judaica section. While leafing through a particular book, he was amazed to find a $100 bill, then another and another!

Clearly, the storeowner was not aware of the treasure hidden in this book. Nevertheless, the young man approached the owner and handed him the money. Later, he was asked what had prompted him to return the money so quickly. "I am a talmid of Rav Pam," was his answer.

At a Minchah minyan in a New York business office, some men were sitting around a table engaged in conversation as they waited for Minchah to begin. When one of the men mentioned someone's name and began to speak lashon hara about him, another man succeeded in changing the conversation by offering a *dvar Torah* (Torah thought). Later, when someone privately expressed his admiration for what the man had accomplished, he replied, "Well, you know where I come from," meaning that he was a talmid of Rav Pam.

Some 60 men were present as Rav Pam's *neshamah* departed this world. One particular man had arrived that night from overseas; on the way home from the airport, he received word to go directly to the hospital. When he arrived there, he found Rav Pam's room filled to capacity. He stood in the hallway, reciting Tehillim and watching what was happening through a glass partition.

As it became clear that the end was nearing, someone said to this man, "You were one of the closest people to Rav Pam — you belong in the room!" But the fellow remained where he was. He later explained: "Before I act, I try to picture how Rav Pam would have done it. I know that it's a great *zechus* to be in the room when a tzaddik is *niftar*. But I also know that if Rav Pam would have been in my position, he would not have pushed his way into the room."

A talmid's father greeted Rav Pam at a wedding and told him, "The Rosh Yeshivah has had such an impact on my son's life." Rav Pam responded, "And your son has had such an impact on *my* life."

It is common to refer to a funeral as the time when the *niftar* (deceased) receives his כָּבוֹד אַחֲרוֹן, *final honor*. Rav Pam once said that a rebbi receives his final honor on the last day of his *talmid's* life, for by living according to his rebbi's teachings, the talmid accords honor to his rebbi until his final day.

Those who follow in Rav Pam's ways can consider themselves his talmidim and will accord honor to his memory throughout their lives.

Let us strive to be his talmidim, now and forever.

PHOTO CREDITS

The following persons and institutions provided photographs and illustrative materials:

Eli Gershbaum
Leonard Greher
Reuven Kaplan
Meir Levy
Shuki Lehrer Photography
Mordechai Mehlman
Rabbi Abish Perlmutter
Rabbi Baruch Rabinowitz
Rabbi Eli Reidel
Rabbi Leibe Wolf
Nachman Wolfson

Agudath Israel of America
Be'er HaGolah Institute
Chinuch Atzmai
Mesivta Torah Vodaath
Nechomas Yisroel
Shuvu
Torah Umesorah
Kalman Zeines Studios
Morgan Studios
Richard Lobell Photography

Many photographs in this book are from the gedolim archives of Moshe D. Yarmish and Tzemach Glenn.